JESUS, MAN OR MYTH?

A Lion Book
an imprint of
Lion Hudson plc
Mayfield House,
256 Banbury Road,
Oxford OX2 7DH, England
www.lionhudson.com
ISBN 0 7459 5147 3

First edition 2005
10 9 8 7 6 5 4 3 2 1 0

Acknowledgments
pp. 16, 32, 34–35, 36, 40–41, 45, 46–47, 49, 52, 55,
69, 72, 77, 78, 103–105, 111, 120, 124, 127, 128,
130, 132, 133, 134, 137, 142, 143, 145, 146, 154, 156
Scripture quotations are from the New Revised Standard
Version published by HarperCollins Publishers, copyright
© 1989 by the Division of Christian Education of the
National Council of the Churches of Christ in the USA,
and are used by permission. All rights reserved.
pp. 60, 63–64, 65, 66, 99 Scripture quotations are from the
Revised English Bible with the Apocrypha copyright © 1989
by Oxford University Press and Cambridge University Press.

A catalogue record for this book is available
from the British Library

Typeset in 13/15 Venetian301 BT

Printed and bound in Great Britain
by Cox & Wyman Ltd

JESUS, MAN OR MYTH?

CARSTEN PETER THIEDE

LION

Publishers' Note

Sadly, the author Carsten Peter Thiede
died during the production of this book.
He had completed the text of the book
but was unable to finish his checking
of final proofs. The publishers have
endeavoured to complete it as accurately
as he would have wished.

CONTENTS

INTRODUCTION

The Jesus of history and the Christ of faith – one and the same or two different persons?

Alone in human history, Jesus of Nazareth did not simply die, rot in a tomb then disappear into the history books or into obscurity. His followers claim that he not only rose from the dead and ascended into heaven, but that he is very much alive today, a real presence in their daily lives and prayers. Critics of Christianity and not a few theologians have tried to come to terms with this two-fold identity by dividing the Jesus of history from the Christ of faith. This Christ of faith, proclaimed by the churches and denominations and experienced by Christians the world over, has been constructed, deconstructed and reconstructed according to the doctrinal decisions of churches and the predilections of synods, committees and individuals. The current debates about controversial, ethical issues are a clear pointer in this direction. The Christ of faith can also be the deeply felt personal Christ of committed men and women who practise what they believe and lead lives that exemplify neighbourly love and the willingness to share the good news as it is recorded in the Gospels and the other twenty-three writings of the New Testament. In some African and Asian countries the risks are high: more Christians have been tortured and killed in the past century than at any other time in history. Believing in the Christ of faith and following him is anything but an academic pursuit.

The Jesus of history, on the other hand, has become a point of conflict between academics who reduce him to snippets of controversial information and others who claim that he is actually the most reliably documented person of antiquity. Still others, somewhere in the middle, claim that we know enough to trust the records but are too far removed from events to prove that they happened as we find them in the New Testament. One simple result of this continuous debate has been mentioned many times, particularly in the media and even from the pulpit: the Jesus of history and the Christ of faith cannot be reconciled. They are two distinct identities, the one to be studied from fragmentary and disputable sources, the other to be proclaimed and believed as best we can.

It should test our sense of irony. Critics and enemies of Christianity quite like the Jesus of history, as it is here that they think they can disprove the claims of the New Testament. Was Jesus born in Bethlehem? Did he rise on the third day? These are solid, historical issues, which many doubters think are the stuff of legend rather than the basis of factual accounts. Conversely, many committed Christians do not like the Jesus of history at all, since they feel it is here that their personal faith may be challenged. Did Jesus really say everything the Gospels record, and did he say it quite like that? Better not to face those questions, or so they think. But the very nature of Jesus and the Christian message leaves no room for choice. The

Jesus of history and the Christ of faith are two inseparable sides of the same coin. Anyone looking at a coin can see only one side at a time. And yet it is obvious that the other, invisible side must exist, for otherwise the coin would be without value. If we look at the Jesus of history, we know that the other side, the Christ of faith, is also there, even though we cannot see it. And if we turn the coin over, the opposite experience applies. We can check that both sides exist, although we look at them separately, gaining different insights from what we see. Anyone who insists that these two sides do not make a whole but must be separated is proclaiming a dangerous falsehood. The message of Jesus Christ is indivisible. It is a message both of history and of faith.

The prevailing attitude of doubt is not a modern phenomenon. Ideological tenets began to gain a foothold in the eighteenth and nineteenth centuries in the guise of post-Enlightenment theories. New philosophies, such as existentialism, offered a quest for meaning after the devastation of the First World War. These tenets changed continental theology beyond recognition. It was no longer intellectually 'correct' to believe in the miracles of Jesus, irrespective of their well-attested historicity, because miracles 'do not happen', and, as one theologian famously put it, it was no longer possible to believe in the resurrection and ascension of Christ in an age of electric shavers. Step by step, historical analysis gave way to the ideology of preconceived ideas about the nature of the Bible and its message. It was an irresistible development that soon focused on the four Gospels. For as long as the Gospels were understood to be what they plainly claim to be, that is, historical stories about a historical person, written – as the earliest records tell us – by eyewitnesses (Matthew and John) or companions and interviewers of eyewitnesses (Mark and Luke), there was no reason to question even those accounts that could not be reconciled with our own everyday experience. Once there had been room for trust and awe, but now this has yielded to a so-called 'hermeneutics of distrust', where faith in the records is seen as naive and doubt is hailed as sincere and scholarly. Of necessity, the Gospels have had to be redated to the period between the seventies and the end of the first century. A pivotal event caused this decision. In AD 30, Jesus predicted the destruction of the Temple; the Romans destroyed it in AD 70. Since Jesus was no longer allowed to be seen as a true prophet, scholars declared that the Gospels must have been written after the event, and they interpreted Jesus' prophecy as a creation of the early church, which wanted Jesus to be seen as the true Son of God rather than an ordinary human being with the gift of the gab. If this looks like a caricature, countless theological publications of the twentieth and early twenty-first centuries unfortunately show that it is not. The results of this reasoning have been taught to students of theology, future parish priests and, as a consequence, to unwitting congregations and pupils in RE classes. Even conservative and evangelical (to use the common labels) Bible and theological colleges have occasionally given in to the temptation of accepting mainstream tendencies rather than facing head on the unhistorical and anti-historical tampering with sources.

To be sure, this is not a question of 'liberal', 'middle-of-the-road', 'conservative' or 'evangelical' scholarship. Labelling opponents merely serves as a convenient detour around serious debates. The quest for the historical Jesus who is also the Christ of faith depends on good scholarship and this may be found across the board. Some readers of this book may remember the excitement in 1976 when John A.T. Robinson published his mould-breaking *Redating the New Testament*. Here was an arch-liberal theologian, labelled by some as the heretic Bishop of Woolwich, allegedly a proponent of the fashionable 'God is dead' tendency, who was suddenly stating, in a well-documented monograph, that every single New Testament text was written before the destruction of the Temple in AD 70. Overnight, he became a traitor to the 'liberal' cause and the new hero of the 'conservatives'. And yet he was and remained the same John A.T. Robinson. He had merely discovered that sober textual scholarship must not be hidden under the bushel of ideological preconception. Take also the prototype of German liberal theology at the turn of the twentieth century, Adolf von Harnack. As a textual historian, he remained a classical scholar to the bone. When he realized that he and his colleagues had placed the Acts of the Apostles much too late in the first century, he corrected his error publicly and stated, in a carefully argued study, that Acts was obviously written before the deaths of James, Peter and Paul – in other words, before AD 62/64. This meant that Luke's Gospel was written earlier still, perhaps as early as the late fifties, and that for those who propose the chronological sequence Mark-Matthew-Luke-Acts, Matthew's and Mark's Gospels must have been written in the fifties of the first century, if not earlier. This was (and is) sensational or provocative only to those who refused to envisage an early Christian community that did the obvious thing and wrote about Jesus, spreading the written message as well as preaching it by word of mouth. In fact, many professional historians have now begun to turn the tables. For many of them, dating the Gospels in the fifties or sixties of the first century is not early at all but still too late. One would have to explain why it took the first Christians twenty, thirty or even up to forty years to produce the earliest written record about Jesus. In other words, dates around the fifties of the first century are the latest conceivable 'middle ground'. John's Gospel, often presented as the odd one out and at best seen as a latecomer, has also been rescued from the dumping ground of second and third-generation datings. Again, it was John A. T. Robinson who set the tone when he advocated a publication date in the late sixties and argued his case persuasively in *The Priority of John* in 1986. Continental scholars like Klaus Berger of Heidelberg University have taken up his baton.

If this means that Jesus was indeed a true prophet, faithfully documented as such – and as much more besides – by the first generation of his followers, this should not come as a surprise. It merely signals the long-overdue return to the results of the first four centuries of Christian scholarship, when people, whose knowledge of the sources was more intimate than ours could possibly be, corroborated the trustworthiness of the historical documents. Needless to say, none of this implies an automatic acceptance of every single tradition about the origins of the New Testament documents. But it does mean that the tide has turned. It is no longer the 'conservatives' and 'traditionalists' who have to prove that our knowledge of Jesus is based on solid and early evidence; it is now the doubting critics who will have to come up with strictly historical propositions, rather than philosophical, ideological ones about the nature and accuracy of the sources.

To put it another way, there is not a shred of evidence of any kind that the Gospels were written later than the mid-first century. They belong to the first generation of witnesses and their disciples – and indeed also to their opponents, who had every opportunity to discredit the Christian claims over some three hundred years until Christianity was given legal status in the Roman empire and slowly acquired the privileges of the imperial religion. But wherever we look, not a single Gospel story is rejected as fantasy or invention in these early centuries. The stories are, at worst, given different interpretations. The philosopher Celsus, for example, one of the opponents who wrote in the mid-second century, does not doubt that Jesus really did perform all his miracles. He merely explains them away as being the result of magic tricks that Jesus had learned as a young boy while he was in Egypt with Mary and Joseph. It sounds risible, but note that Celsus takes the flight into Egypt for granted, something many modern Christian theologians find impossible to do. Or consider another non-Christian, the Jewish-Roman Pharisee, general and historian Flavius Josephus, who wrote during the last third of the first century. He states that Jesus was crucified by Pontius Pilate and that this wise man, 'if indeed one ought to call him a man' (*Jewish*

Antiquities 18:63–64), was the Messiah. Generations of scholars have assumed that a Jew who did not become a Christian could never have called Jesus the Messiah (or Christ, from the Greek). Consequently, the vast majority of interpreters think that this statement at least, if not the whole passage about Jesus, must be a later Christian addition to the original text. But note again that, unlike Christian believers, Josephus does not say that Jesus *is* the Messiah. He says that Jesus *was* the Messiah. And this is something no Christian scribe would have asserted.

So again, here is a non-Christian writer who accepts a basic claim of the Gospels but gives it his own twist. Jesus was more than a mere human being and a wise teacher, he was actually a messiah, but he was the wrong one. Against the majority of Jewish hopes and expectations at the time, he did not come with angelic forces to vanquish both the Roman oppressors and their Jewish collaborators. To Josephus, he was a priestly messiah, one of two or three described in some of the Dead Sea Scrolls as arriving in the last days. However, he was not a warrior who would fight his battles and create a political peace on earth. Josephus, who was still a Jew despite writing from the emperor's palace in Rome, makes his choice. The messiah who came from the Judean desert, who won battles and created peace after the unsuccessful Jewish revolt against the Romans, was none other than the Roman general Vespasian, who was proclaimed Roman emperor in Judea in AD 68. Thus at one stroke, Josephus – like Celsus – accepts and confirms a Gospel account and changes its meaning. But what is most interesting for the historian is the fact that non-Christian authors, even overtly anti-Christian ones like

Celsus, do not attempt to prove the Gospels wrong, even though at this time there was no risk in attacking Christians. This failure to accuse Christians of falsifying their sources is quite remarkable. In fact, Matthew's Gospel reports the earliest known example of an anti-Christian 'retelling' of an event without disputing the central fact, that of the empty tomb on Easter morning.

No one was able to deny the visible, tangible evidence. So what could opponents do? Claim that Jesus staged his disappearance by some magic trick, just as Celsus later tried to explain away the indisputable miracles? The high priest's entourage came up with an even less convincing ploy: they paid the Roman soldiers at the tomb a sizeable amount of money so that they would tell anyone who asked that the disciples had stolen the body while they had been asleep. The high priest even made sure that the Roman prefect would not punish them – bribery was rife in those days, and Pilate was not averse to stealing high-priestly funds (he and Caiaphas even took money from the Temple treasury for the prefect's personal water supply). Again, the ruse was desperate rather than ingenious, but for people who were not prepared to accept the consequences of the bodily resurrection of Jesus, it was worth a try. It was left to some modern theologians to deny that the tomb was empty in the first place, but they could and can only do so by denying the Jewish context of the event. Any Jew who believed in resurrection – and with the exception of the Sadducees, they all did – expected God to grant this to his faithful people in the last days. According to the books of Ezekiel and Daniel and one of the surviving Dead Sea Scrolls, they expected it to be a bodily resurrection. If Jesus was granted a resurrection ahead of other faithful Jews, it still had to be a bodily one for his Jewish followers to believe that it had truly happened. Visions or hallucinations are ruled out in a Jewish context. And it also means that the disciples as much as their opponents had to make sure that the tomb really was empty. To put it another way, the empty tomb is not a proof of resurrection but a precondition – so much so that Paul does not even mention it in his account of the resurrection appearances in his first letter to the Corinthians. It was simply obvious: if the tomb had not been empty, not even Peter, John or James would have been willing to trust in the reality of the resurrection of Jesus.

These are just some examples among many that should help us to understand the background to a number of questions. We are not the first to ask them. The first answers were given by Jesus' contemporaries themselves, who, as it turns out, have provided us with early and reliable sources. In other words, historians have taught us that we must bid farewell to some of the popular myths of New Testament scholarship if we want to get closer to the Jesus of history and the Christ of faith almost two thousand years after these sources were written. These myths have been given impressive names. One of them is 'narrative christology', which basically means that the naive members of the first Christian community were so overwhelmed by their self-induced enthusiasm that they confused the exuberance of their faith in Jesus with historical reality. So they told ('narrated') their stories and what they believed they knew (logos) about Christ. Oddly enough, all the Gospel writers, not just the sober historian Luke, strike the reader as being circumspect writers with a firm grasp of their material, and the editorial postscript to John's Gospel ('This is the disciple who is testifying to these things and has written them, and we know that his testimony is true.' [John 21:24]) flies in the face of all attempts to accuse the first Christians of a kind of theologically mindless intoxication.

Another related myth is known by a German name, *Gemeindetheologie*, which literally means 'community theology'. It is supposed to signify that a large number of blindly enthusiastic, pious but intellectually underdeveloped Christians, who were active in many communities, shaped, extended and often invented stories about Jesus which at some stage were edited by anonymous masterminds. The results of this process of 'redaction' are, allegedly, our four Gospels. Since we have four canonical Gospels that are clearly distinct works of literary history, this process of editorial redaction would have needed to happen four times, independently and chaotically. Not a single trace of such a process has survived, either in the texts or in any papyrus – some of which are from as early as the first century – or in any quote or commentary by early readers. It never happened. The variants in the ancient papyri, the scribal errors and their corrections, marginal notes that crept into the text and many other occurrences that are typical of manuscripts of antiquity (but which occur much less frequently in New Testament papyri than in other classical manuscripts) underline another observation: there never was a second, third or fourth corrected, amended or enlarged edition of any of the Gospels after their first publication. On the contrary, it must be stated, with the confidence of the classical historian and textual critic, that the Gospels were never published in any other form than the one we read today. Singling out the three Gospels of Matthew, Mark and Luke – often called the 'synoptics' because of their 'common view' which arises from their shared material and numerous agreements – we have to acknowledge that they are not the result of an early Christian harmonization, a kind of party handout, but independent writings by independent authors, with differences and variations. To put it bluntly, in the whole realm of classical literature, there is not a single comparable case where a complex history was reported by three authors, writing in different places and with different target groups, and yet agreeing to such a remarkable extent. The moment we accept the Gospels for what they are in literary-historical terms, as outstandingly well-written examples of Greek literature in the Hellenistic period, such observations are anything but sensational. They are obvious. If the all-too-many critics of the Gospels have failed to notice these things, this should tell us more about the critics than about the Gospels.

In a nutshell, then, there is every reason to be confident that the questions we ask today can be answered by looking at the source material written and published by the first followers of Jesus Christ.

I

DID JESUS REALLY EXIST?

Did Caesar exist, for that matter?

How do we know that someone we have never met exists or existed? We owe such knowledge to a combination of factors. First of all, there is the word of people we trust, the 'oral tradition', literally the 'passing on by word of mouth'. Before the invention of newspapers, radio and television, oral tradition was the most common source of information about other people, their existence, words and deeds. Even today, we cannot do without it. When we tell our friends, children or grandchildren about the existence of certain colleagues at our place of work, their names and their characteristics, this is a form of oral tradition. In most cases, there will never be a newspaper report, let alone a papyrus or an inscription, to confirm the truth of our message. The preference for written sources is a relatively modern phenomenon. Most people tend to trust them more than the spoken word — if it isn't in the papers, it hasn't happened. But in antiquity, oral traditions were regarded as equally valid, if not superior, particularly among Jews who had developed a refined technique of memorizing long speeches, poems and prayers (such as the psalms) and teachings (such as the five books of Moses, the 'Torah'). The disciples of Jesus, all of them Jews, would have remembered the comparatively short 'Lord's Prayer' after the first hearing, and the fact that we have two slightly differing versions in Matthew (6:9–13) and Luke (11:2–4) does not mean that these apostles could not remember what Jesus had actually said – it simply means that Jesus gave them two variant versions on two different occasions, a shorter and a longer one, and they remembered them both.

The written sources, if and when they exist, take many forms and can even appear simultaneously with the spoken word. From the third century BC at the latest, Greek-speaking Jews knew a form of shorthand writing. Psalm 45:1 in the Greek translation of the so-called Septuagint uses the term *oxygraphos* for the 'ready scribe', which literally means 'stenographer'. At the time of the New Testament, the Romans too had developed a form of shorthand writing, and the famous philosopher and politician Cicero, who lived in the first century BC, employed his secretary Tiro to record his speeches by using the 'Tironian notes'. In the New Testament itself, we encounter at least one person whose professional qualifications included the ability to write shorthand – the tax official Levi-Matthew, one of the twelve disciples and, according to tradition, the author of a Gospel. Scholars have suggested that Tertius, who 'wrote' Paul's letter to the Romans (Romans 16:22), was another early Christian stenographer. With the exception of a second-century Christian shorthand text on leather, discovered in the

Wadi Murabba'at near the Dead Sea, no early Judeo-Christian notes have survived. Longhand, after all, was the form of writing everyone could read and notes were transcribed as soon as possible. In all likelihood, this is what Matthew did when he wrote his own Gospel using his shorthand notes of the speeches of Jesus to supplement what he found in Mark's model.

The 'lives' of famous people were a frequent feature of classical literature, and quite a few of them have survived in medieval manuscripts. The most famous ones, however, like *Lives of Roman Emperors* by Suetonius and *Parallel Lives* by Plutarchus, were written later than the Gospels. And none of them has survived on papyri. This is in fact a unique feature of the New Testament and its four lives of Jesus. There are now 116 papyri of the New Testament, some 80 of them written within the first two centuries, a few even within decades, of the earthly life of Jesus, and there is not a single literary-historical text from antiquity that comes anywhere near this remarkable textual tradition. Historians will of course use the handful of medieval manuscripts of Tacitus, Suetonius and others, who inform us about the lives of emperors, generals and other heroes of Greco-Roman history. They will make the most of them, relying on their evidence and weighing up conflicting sources. There are, for example, four authors who wrote about the life of the Roman emperor Tiberius, under whom Jesus was crucified by Pontius Pilate – Velleius Paterculus, Tacitus, Suetonius and Cassius Dio. Velleius was a contemporary of Tiberius, Tacitus and Suetonius wrote almost one hundred years after his reign and Cassius Dio two hundred years later. Their accounts often differ considerably and they are far from complete. None of them attempted to produce a complete life story, from cradle to grave, as we would expect to find in a modern biography, and there were of course neither footnotes nor bibliographies. Was Tiberius a good and competent emperor, or was he weak, easily manipulated by Sejanus, the prefect of the Praetorian Guard? Was he one of the greatest soldiers and military commanders the Roman army ever had – as some historians have claimed – or was he a pervert who was despised by the people? The verdict is made difficult by conflicting comments in antiquity, and even today the jury is still out.

Contrast this with the four historical accounts of Jesus, written by four different individuals, for different readers, at different places from Rome to Antioch, but close to the events and to witnesses who could be interviewed. Much like the ancient historiographers who wrote about Emperor Tiberius, the four Gospel authors do not attempt to present complete accounts. Two of them (Mark and John), for example, came to the conclusion that their readers were not interested in a birth story and began with the active years of the adult Jesus. Two (Matthew and Luke) wrote for readers who wanted to know more about the circumstances of Jesus' birth, but their respective aims differed, and so the birth stories in Matthew and Luke highlight different aspects. They are complementary rather than contradictory versions. Professional historians take these nuances in their stride – what matters is not the number of variations, which is, after all, much smaller than that in any other collection of works about the life of a person from antiquity, but the stupendous degree of unanimity.

Throughout this book, we will encounter many examples of their unity in diversity. It has often been remarked that the differences in the detail are not only amazingly minor, compared with other surviving biographies from antiquity, but, more importantly, that they actually underline the trustworthiness of the Gospels. These accounts were not harmonized; no ominously all-powerful church ever erased all the variations or gave in to the temptation of men like Marcion in the mid-second century who suggested that only Luke's Gospel should remain, and even this only in a version expunged of all pro-Jewish tendencies. Intelligent and knowledgeable as the first Christians were, they knew that four different authors ideally do not bore their readers stiff by saying exactly the same things in exactly the same way four times over.

Take the example of the names and number of women at the empty tomb of Jesus. The four authors clearly have their predilections. John mentions only one woman by name, Mary Magdalene. But they all agree that there were women at the tomb. Even John tells his readers that he knows of several other women, for Mary Magdalene runs to two of the disciples and tells them about the experience at the tomb in the first-person plural, 'we' (John 20:2). And the most remarkable agreement is their insistence that the first witnesses were women. The testimony of women did not count in antiquity. It was worthless in court. The apostle Paul, whose intention it was to give the community in Corinth a legally acceptable account of resurrection appearances (1 Corinthians 15:5–8) therefore omits the women altogether and begins with Simon Peter. But the Gospel authors did not write letters with judicially useful data; they wrote history. And thus they had to mention the women. As Jewish men of their time, they would have been embarrassed by all these women as first witnesses; in fact, they may have been happier ignoring them and starting with evidence provided by the men. But they were intent on getting the historical information right, in spite of the social embarrassment involved. And so they all make reference to the women.

In a nutshell, then, the Gospels are not only as historically reliable as other biographies of ancient personalities, but they are quite superior in quality, accuracy and proximity to the events. Like other ancient historical texts, they have a message to proclaim, and this is not the greatness or otherwise of a Roman emperor, but the life, teaching, death and resurrection of the Galilean Jew, Jesus, the Son of God and the Messiah. In the academic mind, there can be no more doubt whatsoever that Jesus existed than did Augustus and Tiberius, the emperors of his lifetime. Even if we assume for a moment that the accounts of non-biblical authors who mention him – Flavius Josephus, Tacitus, Suetonius, Pliny the Younger and others – had not survived, the outstanding quality of the Gospels, Paul's letters and the other New Testament writings is more than good enough for the historian. This does not mean that we have to suspend questioning and accept everything without analysis; nor does it mean that every aspect of Jesus' life can be minutely reconstructed. As we have seen, it was not in the nature of ancient biographies to provide complete data. Thus, we may reconstruct the time of the birth of Jesus as the winter of 7/6 BC, two to three years before the death of Herod the Great, since we know today that the placing of the year 'zero' was based on the miscalculations of a sixth-century monk; but whether it happened on 25 December, 6 January or another day cannot be ascertained. Equally, we know that Jesus was crucified on Friday, 7 April AD 30, as this is the only day when all the chronological data of the Jewish and Roman calendars and the information provided by the Gospels coincide, but since none of the Gospels mentions the exact date unequivocally in modern terms (and why should they?), there are still scholars who think Jesus died in AD 33. As first-century contemporaries, the first readers of the Gospels knew exactly how to understand the chronology. In other words, our difficulty with what we consider to be gaps or ambiguous remarks must not be blamed on the authors. These are entirely our problems. It is not the knowledge of the ancients that is deficient, but ours, two thousand years later. Scholars have estimated that only up to ten per cent of ancient sources – scrolls, inscriptions, imperial coins and so forth – have survived. As any good historian understands, humility, not arrogance, is the attitude of the true scholar. We learn by listening to the surviving sources, not by forcing them into the straitjackets of our preconceptions.

Against this general picture of reliability and widespread attestation, it has been claimed that there is no archaeological evidence for the existence of Jesus. Men like Julius Caesar, Augustus or Tiberius and countless regional rulers and administrators have 'survived' on inscriptions or coins, and there are numerous buildings erected by famous men or dedicated to them. For example, at Caesarea

Maritima, the administrative seat of the Roman prefects and later procurators of Judea, a Latin inscription was found in 1961 that refers to a 'Tiberieum' and to 'Pontius Pilate' as 'prefect of Judea'. Scholars continue to discuss the precise nature of the 'Tiberieum' – was it a temple or a lighthouse? – but it certainly was dedicated to the Emperor Tiberius, for the Latin ending '-eum' signifies a public building erected in honour of the person mentioned. Thus, the word 'Augusteum' usually describes a temple of Emperor Augustus. The 'Tiberieum' at Caesarea Maritima was built by Pontius Pilate, and because his title is given as 'prefect', we can correct the erroneous reference to Pilate as a 'procurator' given by the Roman historian Tacitus. The governors of Judea were promoted from the rank of the (military) prefect to that of the (civilian) procurator only later, under Emperor Claudius. Felix and Festus, the two governors who interrogated the apostle Paul at Caesarea, were already procurators. In other words, an inscription can provide useful information, corroborative detail and circumstantial evidence. From the lifetime of Jesus, on the other hand, no coins, inscriptions or buildings have survived that carry his name. So is this an argument against the importance of Jesus as a historical figure, or even against his existence?

One thing is certain. Before Jesus, no historian had written about the life of a carpenter's adopted son. And in mere human terms, this is what Jesus was in the eyes of the world. Seen like this, the Gospels were a breakthrough in world literature. Remember that emperors, governors and great heroes of politics and warfare were praised in works of history, but no Greek or Roman historian would have considered a Jewish craftsman from an eastern province, executed according to Roman law, the rightful subject of historiography. And who would have minted coins bearing his name? It would have been illegal, anyway. Temples were inconceivable too. The Romans had temples built in honour of their emperors. They were part of the 'imperial cult' and three have been excavated in Israel dedicated to the 'Son of God', Augustus. All three of them were built by Herod the Great, at Caesarea Maritima, Caesarea Philippi and Samaria/Sebaste. But a temple of Jesus? The first churches, recognizable as separate buildings rather than house churches in private homes, were built in the late third century, at Dura Europos and at Silchester near Reading, just before the devastating persecution of Christians under Emperor Diocletian. It was his successor Constantine, called the Great, who allowed Christians to start an empire-wide building programme.

Even so, there are two noteworthy exceptions: on the southwestern hill of Jerusalem, today's Mount Zion, the so-called 'Tomb of David' is not actually King David's tomb (the unknown site was somewhere in the Ofel region, in what is now the Arab village of Silwan, probably not far from the pool of Siloah). It is a very early Christian synagogue, built by Jewish Christians who had returned from voluntary exile in Pella (modern Jordan) after the Jewish revolt against the Romans. Emperor Vespasian had given them permission to resettle in the devastated city of Jerusalem, because of all the Jews they alone had not revolted. They returned to their old living quarters, and, on the site of their traditional meeting place, the 'upper room', they built a synagogue church. If you go there today with a compass in your hand, you will notice that the niche for the Torah scrolls is not directed towards Temple Mount, as it should be in a Jewish synagogue in Jerusalem, but towards Golgotha and the empty tomb. The builders were Jewish Christians, and the stones they used for the outer walls, still visible today, came from the spoils of the Temple. Underneath the present-day floor of the building, first-century graffiti was discovered that names Jesus and invokes his name in prayer. These inscriptions are not visible any longer, as the synagogue church is being used by an ultra-orthodox Jewish minority movement, but they have been recorded and published.

The second exception is a fragment of the headboard from the cross of Jesus which survives in a side chapel of a church in Rome, built above the palace of Helena, Emperor Constantine's mother. Helena discovered this headboard when she visited Jerusalem in AD 328, and she ordered that Hadrian's temple to Venus should be pulled down in order to reach the remains of Golgotha underneath. She had it cut into three parts, giving one to her son Constantine in Byzantium, leaving one in Jerusalem (where it remained on display until the seventh-century when it was stolen and probably destroyed by the Persians) and taking one back with her to her palace in Rome, where it remains. Her Sessorian Palace, now called 'Santa Croce in Gerusalemme', houses the fragment on which there is an inscription which reads, in Hebrew, Greek and Latin: '[Jesus of] Nazareth K[ing of the Jews]'. Recent research has shown that it is not a forgery, and that the last line was copied from Pilate's own orders, in correct, bureaucratic Latin. The prefect would not have written all three lines himself. He would have given the scribe a piece of papyrus with the official, legally binding Latin version and left the rest to the servant.

Thus we do have two early archaeological finds after all: this fragment from the headboard, made in the early hours of 7 April AD 30, and those recordings of the name of Jesus beneath the surface of the so-called Tomb of David, the first Jewish-Christian synagogue church, from the mid-seventies AD. The latter is a form of Christian evidence; the former is a Roman document, made on behalf of the same prefect Pontius Pilate whose inscription at Caesarea Maritima is the only non-literary evidence that Jesus ever existed.

And this is the punchline: for the historian, the literary evidence and the textual sources are always more important than archaeological discoveries. Scholars knew about Pontius Pilate and had no doubt that he existed even before the discovery of his inscription in 1961. It has become a popular tendency to trust in archaeological finds rather than in the primary sources, the texts themselves. Not long ago, there was a worldwide commotion about the so-called 'Ossuary of James', a bone casket with an Aramaic text that read 'James, Son of Joseph, Brother of Jesus'. This, according to some excited commentators, was the first archaeological proof that Jesus ever existed. But serious observers immediately asked: Jesus who? James, Joseph and Jesus were among the six most popular Jewish names in the first century, and in Jerusalem alone, there were about a dozen families with a James whose father was called Joseph and whose brother was called Jesus. Even in the New Testament, there are four different people called Jesus. Unless specific information was added, such as '(brother of) Jesus the Messiah' or '(half-brother of) Jesus of Nazareth', the inscription is useless. After all, even Pilate made sure that everyone knew which Jesus he crucified by writing 'Jesus of Nazareth' rather than merely 'Jesus'. Or, to put it another way, the bone casket tells us much less about the one Jesus who was the Christ than what we already know about him from our primary sources, the Gospels, and the whole New Testament, Flavius Josephus and so forth. In the meantime, it has turned out that the ossuary is a forgery anyway. But even if it had been authentic, the lesson to be learned would have been the same. Here we return to the beginning of this chapter: archaeology, coins, inscriptions and buildings may offer helpful information, but the Gospels, as four independent, historical documents, are the safe and reliable groundwork. As literary-historical sources, they prove the existence of Jesus as conclusively as Suetonius, Tacitus and the others prove the existence of the emperors Augustus and Tiberius.

2

HOW DO WE KNOW THE STORIES ABOUT JESUS ARE ACTUALLY TRUE?

How do we know any story about a person from antiquity is true?

In the previous chapters, we have looked at questions of history and textual transmission. In this chapter, the perspective shifts to aspects that may appear technical at first but which apply to all accounts that have survived from antiquity. We have established that the textual tradition of the New Testament is beyond compare, and we have seen that there is no reason to doubt the existence of Jesus. But what about the deeds ascribed to him, and the general reliability of biographies about famous – and sometimes infamous – people from antiquity? As far as Jesus is concerned, our sources are adamant: we are dealing with stories told and passed on by eyewitnesses and their associates.

To be sure, eyewitnesses are not infallible. Then, as now,

their memories may have been selective, even deficient as far as particular details are concerned. But they remain eyewitnesses, and this makes them guarantors of the fact that an event took place at all. The first Christians were fully aware of this distinction. They realized at a glance that, despite the common ground, there were real differences between the Gospel accounts. For example, did Jesus heal the Roman centurion's servant at Capernaum when the centurion came and asked him for help, and did he do so without walking towards the garrison (Matthew 8:5–13)? Or did the centurion, a friend of the Jewish community, send some of the Jewish elders to Jesus, followed by a further group of friends when Jesus was approaching the garrison (Luke 7:1–10)? Who told this story to whom, initially? Luke was not an eyewitness himself, but he had access to eyewitness material (Luke 1:1–2) and probably interviewed people like Mary, James and Cleopas and many others. Matthew, on the other hand, only became an eyewitness later on, because, according to a tradition that modern research has reaffirmed, he is to be identified with the disciple Levi-Matthew; but at the stage of this healing, he had not yet joined the circle of the twelve and had to rely on others to tell him what had happened. Could those informing Matthew and Luke really have differed on what to us is one of the most striking early miracles of Jesus?

The answer, of course, is 'yes'. Years later, when they were interviewed, it did not matter to them how Jesus was asked to heal the servant, or whether he was walking in the direction of the garrison when the news reached the group that the servant had been healed. The sources agree that it was a 'long-distance' healing, where Jesus neither saw nor touched the sick person. And what mattered, historically speaking, was the fact that Jesus had healed the servant of an officer of the Roman army. Many Jews despised the Romans. They were the pagan occupiers who venerated their emperor as a god. The zealots, always ready to fight the Romans, had their headquarters not far from Capernaum, at the fortress of Gamla, and one of them, Simon the Zealot, had become one of the twelve disciples. Had Jesus chosen him to make sure that the zealots learned the lesson of loving even one's enemies? The healing of the centurion's servant was a case in point. And both Matthew and Luke emphasize that Jesus praises the Roman officer's faith in the healing power of the Messiah: 'Truly, I tell you, in no one in Israel have I found such faith' (Matthew 8:10); 'I tell you, I have not found such faith in Israel' (Luke 7:9). The message and the punchline of each version of the story are the same, and the very fact that there are these differences in peripheral detail indicates that the church did not tamper with the sources. No one 'streamlined' them so as to smooth over the personal nuances and to make them word-identical.

Put another way, eyewitnesses remain primary sources of information, warts and all, and the first Christians knew how vital this was for the credibility of their proclamation even before the first Gospel was written. After the suicide of Judas, a new twelfth disciple had to be chosen; twelve, after all, was the number determined by Jesus. James, 'the brother of the Lord' (Galatians 1:19), who was not one of the twelve, later underlines the symbolic value of the number when he addresses his letter to 'the twelve tribes in the diaspora', or, in other words, to *all* followers of Christ who were dispersed throughout the the Roman empire, to Jewish and Gentile Christians alike. They, like the original twelve tribes of Israel, had become God's chosen people. Thus, the election of a new twelfth disciple to succeed Judas was no small matter. But whom to choose, and how? Most readers of the book of Acts remember the story (Acts 1:15–26) because the decision is made by the casting of lots. It remained a unique incident in early Christianity, because a few weeks later, after the coming of the Holy Spirit at Pentecost, such a 'technical' device was no longer necessary. Historically speaking, what should really strike the reader is the fact that only two candidates came forward, Joseph Barsabbas, also known by the Latin name Justus, and Matthias. The lot fell on Matthias, but the other person's name was not forgotten. Why? Because he, too, fulfilled the one criterion that truly mattered: 'So one of the men who have accompanied us throughout the time that the Lord Jesus went in and out among us, beginning from the baptism of John until the day when he was taken up from us – one of these must become a witness with us to his resurrection,' Peter explained. This was decisive: the new twelfth disciple had to have been an eyewitness to everything from the very first day of Jesus' public appearance. And this is all the more remarkable as not even all of the original twelve fulfilled this criterion – Judas, for example, had not been among those who had witnessed the baptism of Jesus, and nor had Matthew-Levi, the Gospel author-to-be. The first Christian community realized that the scepticism of Jewish opponents, and of the Gentiles they lived among, could only be overcome by an unflinching insistence on the historical facts. In the choosing of the successor to Judas, nothing else would do. Only two candidates qualified. And 'the lot is cast into the lap, but the decision is the Lord's alone' (Proverbs 16:33).

Matthias and the twelve were oral witnesses. In other words, they proclaimed what they had seen and understood by word of mouth, in public gatherings, at or near the Temple, in synagogues and in private conversation. Almost simultaneously, the first written sources came into being. As we saw in the previous chapters, scholars have agreed to differ about the dates of the Gospels, but experts in classical literature and history in particular have come to prefer early dates, preceding the destruction of the Temple in AD 70. One line of argument that has been cited in this context concerns the reality of early Christian life. The authorized core group of eyewitnesses was limited to twelve, and although others, such as the deacon Philip who baptized the first non-Jewish convert – the financial secretary of the Nubian Queen Mother (Acts 6:6; 8:26–39), were called by the Lord to help, the immediate success of their ministry soon surpassed their means. They simply could not be everywhere to proclaim the good news in person. It was a situation fraught with risks: incomplete or even false teachings could develop unchallenged. Peter and, later, Paul spent much of their time travelling and writing to combat these developments. Paul's letters in particular are meant to correct errors and to put local communities back on the right track. In one of his letters, Paul explicitly asks for his teaching to be passed on to others and to make sure that they read what he had written elsewhere (Colossians 4:15–16). Written records were needed, and there are scholars today who are convinced that at least one Gospel, Mark's, existed when Paul wrote his letters, and that another one, Luke's, may have been known to him in his later years. Indeed, it looks as though Paul assumes his readers knew the Gospel accounts, so that he did not have to refer to the life, public sermons and miracles of Jesus to any great extent. In one instance, it looks as though his preaching was even checked against written records. In Berea, the Jewish community listened to him and 'examined the scriptures every day to see if these things were so' (Acts 17:11).

In the Greek text of Acts, the plural 'scriptures' is used. As a rule, New Testament writings use the singular, 'scripture', when they mean the Torah – the five books of Moses – and the Prophets. The plural is used when other writings, even those outside the generally accepted canon, are included. Thus, the Jews at Berea compared the oral teaching of Paul to a wide-ranging collection of texts in the library of their synagogue, not just to the books of what we have come to call the Old Testament. First of all, they would have compared Paul's interpretation to the Hebrew Bible. It was a process that was common among Jews. Any new teaching had to be judged by the yardstick of the Torah. Jesus himself, recently risen from the dead, applies this method on the road to Emmaus. When the two disciples he meets on that road fail to understand what had happened on Easter morning, he says: '"Oh, how foolish you are, and how slow of heart to believe all that the prophets have declared! Was it not necessary that the

Messiah should suffer these things and then enter into his glory?" Then, beginning with Moses and all the prophets, he interpreted to them the things about himself in all the scriptures' (Luke 24:25–27). The second stage, for those who wanted to pursue their studies, and usually identified by the plural 'scriptures', would have included further Jewish writings. Some of these writings were quoted and alluded to in the New Testament. For example, Jude in his short letter quotes from the popular book of Enoch (Jude 4, 6, 14–15). In the eyes of a Jewish community like the one at Berea, a book like Mark's would not yet have been a 'Gospel', or part of the New Testament or of the literature of the Christian church – these were categories that came into being decades later. They would have read it as a Jewish text, written by a Jew about a Jew, primarily for other Jews, proclaiming the identity of the Jewish Messiah.

Messianic hope was rife in those days, and a text about a man whom his Jewish followers venerated as the Messiah in spite of his crucifixion by the Romans could not be ignored. Not least, opponents had to scrutinize the first writings of this new Jewish movement. If you want to fight an enemy effectively, you have to know his 'philosophy', message and strategy. And if we abandon the implausibly late dates commonly suggested for the publication of the Gospels and accept the date of AD 40 suggested for Mark's Gospel by the Jewish classical philologist Guenther Zuntz, or the mid to late forties preferred by other philologists and historians, we can see how soon this Jewish messianic document could have reached synagogal libraries throughout the Roman empire. It looks as though it even reached the library of the orthodox messianic movement of the Essenes at Qumran, where, according to a group of Jewish and non-Jewish scholars, a fragment of Mark's Gospel was found in Cave Seven. The people who collected these writings did it for a purpose. They wanted to read, study, compare and make up their own minds about the ways of God and his Messiah with his people. As for Paul, he was no eyewitness to the years prior to the crucifixion. It may have seemed advisable to the Jews at Berea – and elsewhere – to read written records, in order to establish whether the stories told about Jesus were actually true and whether they harmonized with the ancient prophecies.

There is a contemporary parallel to this practice. Among the four major Jewish movements of the decades before the destruction of the Temple in AD 70 – the Sadducees, Pharisees, Essenes and Christians – three were known to reach out to Jews and non-Jews through active missionary activities. Only the Sadducees were apparently content with their role as the Temple priesthood, which involved thousands of auxiliary priests all over the country – of whom Zechariah, John the Baptist's father, was one (Luke 1: 8–9) – and which formed the majority group in the legal council, the Sanhedrin. The Pharisees and the Essenes, on the other hand, did their missionary work everywhere in Judea, Samaria and Galilee, and even outside the Jewish homeland. Essene manuscripts – today known as the Dead Sea Scrolls – reached Rome, Alexandria, ancient Cairo and many other cities. And the Pharisees were present in all the major cities with Jewish quarters, including the city of Tarsus in Asia Minor, where Paul was born (Acts 23:6). Nothing of what the Sadducees and the

Pharisees may have written in those years has survived. The Sadducees and the Essenes disappeared from history after the destruction of Jerusalem and its Temple and the occupation of Qumran by the Romans, but the Pharisees carried on and created an enormous library of texts, culminating in the Mishnah, the Jerusalem and the Babylonian Talmuds. These collections may include ancient material, going back to the time of Jesus and earlier, but they were published in their present state as late as the sixth century. This state of affairs leaves us with just two 'libraries' from the first century, the Essene study library in the caves near Qumran and the twenty-seven writings that were later incorporated into the collection known as the New Testament. The Essene literature was written between about 160 BC and, at the latest, AD 68, when the Roman tenth legion occupied Qumran and the area of the caves. The twenty-seven writings of the New Testament obviously came later, some time after the death and resurrection of Jesus in AD 30, but they were concluded just before AD 70. Thus, the final writings of both libraries were produced simultaneously.

What does this mean? It means, of course, that both movements not only knew of each other but also studied each other's texts to find out where they differed and where they agreed. What is more, the Jews who followed Jesus the Christ learned some useful practical lessons. The older messianic movement, the Essenes, had sent their adherents, trained at Qumran and in Jerusalem, into the villages and towns to establish families and visibly live the Essene way of life as an example to others. And, most significantly, they did not leave it at that. They certainly hoped for the Messiah to come at any moment, yet they took the time to write about their hopes and expectations and developed a refined system of rules and a new form of scriptural interpretation, called 'Pesharim' in Hebrew. Missionary preaching and living were accompanied by missionary writing. For the first Christians, the consequences were plain – they could not seriously hope to persuade other Jews of the superiority of their own message, and the truth of the Messiah Jesus, if they did not at least employ the same means successfully applied by the Essenes: preaching, writing and living as a committed community. Many introductions to the New Testament still assume that the first Christians only began to write when their fervent hopes for the immediate return of the Messiah Jesus were disappointed. It is far from certain that the majority of first-generation Christians ever held such a belief. Paul, for example, who may initially have hoped for an early return, warned against hasty speculations in his earliest letter, I Thessalonians (5:1–11).

Yet even a community like the Essenes, who prayed and wished for the immediate arrival of the Messiah, did not retire into their homes to sit and wait. They wrote scroll after scroll, copied them and sent them out into the Jewish world. For the first Jewish Christians, writing about Jesus therefore became an immediate imperative. It was not good enough just to match the Essenes' messianic scrolls with oral messages. If the going got tough and evidence from the scriptures was sought, then scroll had to be placed next to scroll, the Torah and the Prophets next to the 'Habakuk Pesher' from Qumran (to name just one example) and the Gospel of Mark – or any of the other early Jewish-Christian texts. Here, the Christians had a distinct advantage. Their texts were based on eyewitness accounts. In many respects, the Essenes followed their 'Teacher of Righteousness' and a document he may have written himself, 'Miqsat Ma'ase ha-Torah' ('Something about the doing of the Torah'), but they never venerated this teacher as the Messiah, nor was any eyewitness to his actions in the second century BC still alive when the eyewitnesses of Jesus' ministry told their story. It was an important claim of the early Christians, handed down as a fixed tradition, that all four Gospels were as good as the personal presence of the twelve apostles themselves. John claims that he himself was such an eyewitness (John 19:35) and the Johannine community responsible for the publication of his Gospel confirms this (John 21:24). Luke interviewed eyewitnesses and researched and compared earlier written sources (Luke 1:1–4). According to the earliest available tradition – which has been corroborated by modern research – Matthew was the disciple Levi-Matthew, an eyewitness. And Mark, or so we read in the ancient tradition about his Gospel, was the trusted friend and interpreter of the eyewitness Simon Peter.

The apostle Peter himself realized the importance of eyewitness testimonies: in his second letter, which has wrongly been classified as inauthentic by many modern scholars, he insists on the difference between myth and truth: 'For we did not follow cleverly devised myths', he declares (2 Peter 1:16–18), 'when we made known to you the power and coming of our Lord Jesus Christ, but we had been eyewitnesses of his majesty. For he received honour and glory from God the Father when that voice was conveyed to him by the majestic glory, saying, "This is my Son, my Beloved, with whom I am well pleased." We ourselves heard this voice come from heaven, while we were with him on the holy mountain.' Here, Peter refers to the transfiguration of Christ, as Mark reports it in his Gospel (Mark 9:2–13). He chooses this particular example because it links Jesus to Moses and Elijah – his forerunners – and to God's authoritative voice, and also because it is precisely one of those incidents that people even then may have put aside as legendary. No, Peter says, it is the historical truth; it really did happen; I saw it; I was there.

A common word for eyewitnesses, 'watchers', in Greek literature is *epóptai*. It is used here in 2 Peter 1:16, and it also occurs in Greek mystery cults, where it signifies the status of those who were admitted to the highest grade, to watch secret goings-on. Again, Peter underlines the special status of Christianity: the truth of Jesus is not hidden, but revealed; it is not entrusted to a select group of initiates, but to everyone who decides to trust the historical message.

Let us conclude this chapter with a look at a passage that occurs in Matthew's and Luke's Gospels (Matthew 11:2–6; Luke 7:18–23). Jesus answers the definitive question of John the Baptist who, imprisoned by Herod Antipas, had sent two of his disciples to ask, 'Are you the one who is to come, or are we to wait for another?' How can Jesus prove to John that he really is the Messiah, and that John, expecting certain death on the fortress of Machaerus, east of the Dead Sea, had prophesied correctly? 'Go and tell John what you have seen and heard,' Jesus replies. John's disciples are not supposed to convey a subtle theological exposition – their own eyewitness account is all that will matter to John. The list is impressive enough: 'The blind receive their sight, the lame walk, the lepers are cleansed, the deaf hear, the dead are raised, the poor have good news brought to them.' It is a list of five miracles, followed by a statement about Jesus' preaching ministry. All these points could be found in the book of Jeremiah and in a more recent Dead Sea Scroll (4Q521). They were the so-called messianic miracles, described more fully in Chapter 5. Only the Messiah would perform them; many people, including disciples of John, had seen them.

To underline the uniqueness of his messiahship (after all, the Essenes, for example, expected more than one messiah), Jesus adds a miracle that does not occur in the messianic miracle lists of Jeremiah and Qumran: 'The lepers are cleansed.' Not far from Capernaum, Jesus had done just this (Matthew 8:1–4; Mark 1:40–45, Luke 5:12–16) and it was a sensation. No Jew, let alone a teacher and rabbi, would go anywhere near a leper. They were the untouchables of Jewish society. But Jesus not only allowed the man to approach him, he healed him by touching the contagious skin. And as if this was not enough, he placed this healing in the centre of his five miracles: the blind receive their sight, the lame walk, the lepers are cleansed, the deaf hear, the dead are raised. The messianic society of Jesus is a revolutionary one. Those who are considered outcasts everywhere else will take centre stage in his community. Again, this is not theory, but practice. Eyewitnesses saw it happen, and Jesus invites them to understand what they have seen.

Eyewitness accounts may differ in many details. They did so in antiquity and they do so today. Such variations are to be expected. What matters to the historian, who has to decide if an account is trustworthy or not, is the overall picture. In other words, the question to be answered is did an event happen, and not were there two people healed or one, did they sit or stand, and so forth. Eyewitness accounts are important sources and the historian is grateful if they exist. Given the outstanding reliability of the Gospels as literary sources, as we saw in previous chapters, this further strengthens the argument that the stories about Jesus are actually true. In Chapter 7, which looks at the resurrection, we will consider this type of evidence from yet another angle. Suffice it to say, at this stage, the reluctance of modern, post-Enlightenment people to accept the historical reality of events they cannot comprehend is no yardstick for measuring reliability in classical history. Sometimes we just have to learn humility and understand that an ancient text may know more than we do.

3

HOW WAS JESUS BORN?

And where?

Gone are the days when people doubted that Jesus ever existed. But in antiquity, details of birth, birthplace, childhood and youth were not considered vital information. What mattered were the years of public action, spanning the period of the early career through triumph to – often – heroic death. Sometimes, an author assumed that the circumstances of birth were of interest to his readers and so he wrote about them. Readers of the New Testament are in a privileged position: not one, but two of the four Gospel authors, Matthew and Luke, report the birth of Jesus, and what is more, they do so from different perspectives. This means they did not copy each other or quote from one and the same source but that they must have had access to a pool of information from which they chose what to present to their readers. Furthermore, as we suggested earlier, Luke, the investigator, would have interviewed the one person who knew precisely what had taken place: Mary, the mother of Jesus, herself.

Modern minds refuse to accept the unanimous verdict

of Matthew and Luke: Jesus was born without a human father. How can this be? they ask, and they merely put the question as Mary had asked it herself when God's angel (*ángelos* in Greek, which literally means 'messenger') went to Nazareth and told her, 'And now, you will conceive in your womb and bear a son, and you will name him Jesus.' Mary said to the angel, 'How can this be, since I am a virgin?' (Luke 1:31, 34). She must have been as perplexed as readers have been ever since, and the explanation given by the angel was not meant to satisfy gynaecologists: 'The Holy Spirit will come over you, and the power of the Most High will overshadow you; therefore the child to be born will be holy; he will be called Son of God.' Nothing like it had happened before in human history, although some desperate New Testament critics have claimed, wrongly, that gods and sons of gods were born similarly in pagan antiquity. Mary and her fiancé Joseph could not simply nod and say, 'Well, we are not sure why it has to be us, but we are not the first.' They had to come to terms with a unique event and, in Jewish society, it was a situation fraught with potentially lethal danger. A child born outside or before marriage was illegitimate, and the mother was likely to be stoned to death as a fornicator or adulterer. Joseph, the devout Jew who had not slept with Mary, was entitled to cast her out and leave her to her fate. He, too, needed some rather persuasive arguments to keep her, marry her and accept the child she was about to give birth to (Matthew 1:19–25). Only after the birth of Jesus did they consummate their marriage (Matthew 1:25). Mary and the two Gospel authors do not even try to explain the biological connotations. Zoologists have pointed out that the phenomenon of 'parthenogenesis', birth without male physical involvement, is known in the animal world, but we can be sure that Mary and Joseph would not have breathed a sigh of relief if they had known about this phenomenon. They trusted God and took rumours about the birth in their stride. There was nothing anyone could do to them, as Joseph had legitimized Jesus by marrying Mary and adopting her son, an adminstrative act which also invested him with the messianic lineage of David (Luke 3:23; Matthew 1:16).

The apostle Paul later notes that Mary herself was of Davidic descent. In Romans 1:3 he writes that Jesus was 'descended from David according to the flesh', meaning on the human side, through Mary. And Mary had another ancestral line to offer her son: according to Luke 1:5 and 1:36, she was a close relative of Elizabeth, the mother of John the Baptist, who was a descendant of Aaron, the brother of Moses. In other words, Mary probably was an Aaronite herself. And since many Jews in those days, the Essenes among them, expected the Messiah to be either a descendant of David (this was the majority position) or of Aaron, or perhaps even both, Jesus was born with a multiple pedigree: the Son of God, the son of the Aaronic and Davidic Mary, and the adoptive son of Joseph, a descendant of King David. Christians later pointed to 2 Samuel 7:12–14, where the prophet Nathan gives David the divine promise: 'When your days are fulfilled and you lie down with your ancestors, I will raise up your offspring after you, who shall come forth from your body, and I will establish his kingdom. He shall build a house for my name, and I will establish the throne of his kingdom forever. I will be a father to him, and he shall be a son to me.' The anonymous letter to the Hebrews, written in the sixties of the first century AD, provides an early example of this prophetic thinking among the first generation of Jewish Christians: 'He (God's Son) is the reflection of God's glory and the exact imprint of God's very being, and he sustains all things by his powerful word. When he had made purification for sins, he sat down at the right hand of the Majesty on high, having become as much superior to angels as the name he has inherited is more excellent than theirs. For to which of the angels did God ever say, "You are my Son, today I have begotten you"? Or again, "I will be his Father, and he will be my Son"?' (Hebrews 1:3–5).

Against all this, doubters and opponents never had a chance. 'I can't believe it,' or 'It goes against the laws of nature,' or 'It can't be repeated by experiment and therefore never happened,' and similar subterfuges of the modern mind are unacceptable as historical criteria. In late antiquity, opponents of Christianity came up with a theory that is as ludicrous as it is polemical: Mary was raped by a Roman soldier named something like Pandera or Panthera. Tell this to a professional historian of classical times and you will provide him or her with a moment of comic relief amid the serious study of sources.

Matthew provides us with an additional perspective (1:23). Always keen to find an explanation for any striking event somewhere in the prophetic writings, he noticed Isaiah 7:13–14, where we read: 'Then Isaiah said: "Hear then, O house of David! Is it too little for you to weary mortals, that you weary my God also? Therefore the Lord himself will give you a sign. Look, a virgin is with child and shall bear a son, whom she will name God is with us (Immanuel)."' Critics have asserted that 'virgin' should be 'young woman', and some modern translations have relegated the 'virgin' to the footnotes. The Hebrew word is *alma*, which signifies a young, unmarried woman of childbearing age. Given the social culture of Isaiah's days, she was therefore either a virgin or a prostitute. Since the context of Isaiah's prophecy rules out the prostitute, we are left with the virgin. There is another Hebrew word, *betula*, which means virgin in a neutral, biological sense. An unmarried woman in her eighties could be called a *betula*, but she could not be an *alma*, because she was beyond the age of conception. Since Isaiah's prophecy is about the birth of a son who will be God among his people, 'God with us', he had to use the Hebrew *alma*. In the third century BC, when Jews in the region of Alexandria translated the Hebrew Bible into Greek for the growing number of fellow Jews who no longer knew Hebrew well enough to study and understand the original text, they had to decide which Greek expression to use for Isaiah's *alma*. Was it to be 'a young woman' or 'a virgin'? They opted for *parthénos*, virgin. Some two hundred years before the birth of Jesus, Jews who translated the Bible for other Jews understood Isaiah correctly. And Matthew, who wrote his Gospel in Greek, quotes from that Greek translation, known as the Septuagint, relying on the accuracy and understanding of those translators, and, needless to say, on the information he had received from Mary and her circle.

As if this were not enough, the place where Jesus was born has also been brought into question. Viewed superficially, Bethlehem looks unlikely. After all, we know Jesus as Jesus of Nazareth, not Jesus of Bethlehem. When Pontius Pilate, following Roman custom, ordered a headboard, the *titulus*, to be attached to the cross, it read 'Jesus of Nazareth, King of the Jews'. John was one of those who were fully aware of this shift in emphasis. In his Gospel, he mentions a group of Jews who rejected Jesus and said, 'Surely the Messiah does not come from Galilee, does he? Has not the Scripture said that the Messiah is descended from David and comes from Bethlehem, the village where David lived?' (John 7:41–42). By AD 29, some 35 years after Jesus' birth, public knowledge of his birthplace had disappeared. Jesus had been a Nazarene for more than three decades, and this was how everyone knew him. He did not walk about advertising his birthplace or his two-fold Davidic descent from Mary and his adoptive father Joseph, so even his messianic family tree was not known to Jews in Jerusalem. Jesus, as we saw, worked and convinced through his actions, his miracles, his preaching, his whole way of life. The Jesus who did not quote scripture to convince the imprisoned John the Baptist of his true messiahship, but pointed to the miracles he had performed, was the same Jesus who did not have to proclaim Bethlehem and his human ancestry back to David and Aaron.

After the resurrection, on the road to Emmaus, he pulled all the strings of evidence together, and, 'beginning with Moses and all the prophets, he interpreted to them the things about himself in all the Scriptures' (Luke 24:27). But this was later, on Easter Day, and he was in conversation with two disciples. With others, with the crowds, Jesus' strategy was a different one. In fact, Matthew only mentions these things because they make sense in the context of his general approach – the historical events should be understood within the framework of prophecy. Modern readers of his Gospel have all too often misunderstood his procedure. Matthew, so they thought, happened upon a useful messianic prophecy and then invented a place or an event to fit it. The opposite is true, of course. First, there was the event, then there was the search for the fitting prophecy. This is highlighted by the way he tells the story of Bethlehem, the wise men from the east, King Herod and his scribes (Matthew 2:1–12). First, he states that the birth had taken place in Bethlehem of Judea, a matter-of-fact piece of information, helpful to those who may have known that there was another Bethlehem, a tiny hamlet in Galilee. Then he introduces the wise men. He does not call them kings, nor does he say that there were three – these are later, early-medieval accretions to his account, based on the assumption that three kinds of gifts, gold, frankincense and myrrh, presuppose three givers, and that they were so valuable that the men just had to be kings. We simply do not know how many of them there were. Matthew calls them *magoi*, which in those days was a technical term for astronomers and astrologers, two professions that went hand-in-hand in classical antiquity. And he adds that they came *apò anatolôn*, which means 'from the orient, from the east'. Archaeologists and experts in near-eastern astronomy have established that there was a world-famous observatory called Sippar near Babylon. Cuneiform clay tablets have been found bearing

calculations of stellar movements for the years 7 and 6
BC. They predicted a near-conjunction of Jupiter and
Saturn over Judea, and, as interpreters of their own
calculations, the astronomers expected this to herald the
birth of a saviour of the world. Many peoples, from the
Egyptians to the Romans, had expected a saviour to arrive
in their day; Virgil, the Roman poet, wrote one of his most
famous poems, the fourth eclogue, about such
expectations, but he was vague enough to give rise to
numerous speculations about the person he may have
meant. Some thought he had been thinking of Emperor
Augustus; others, in the Middle Ages, praised Virgil as a
prophet of Christ, and his statue was placed next to those
of Isaiah and Jeremiah in the Spanish cathedral of
Zamorra. In other words, the 'magoi from the east' were not
alone in their hopes and stargazings, but they were
sufficiently convinced to travel west, following the
movement of the stars. This is where Matthew picks up
the story.

The men arrive in Jerusalem, the capital of Judea, to
find out where exactly the saviour king was born. Herod, a
keen observer of the stars himself, hears about their
enquiries and is frightened. Could a rival to his own rule
and dynastic plans, a saviour, and thus, in Jewish terms, a
messiah, have been born under his nose? Knowledgeable
about prophecies and stars as he is, the thought that this
future rival could have been born in Bethlehem does not
occur to him (Matthew 2:3–4). This is important
information: Bethlehem was not on the map of messianic
expectations before the birth of Jesus. Herod did not know
about it. The Dead Sea Scrolls, from the library of the

Essene Community at Qumran, a community that, as we saw, was eagerly expecting the Messiah, do not mention Bethlehem once in this context. Herod calls for the chief priests and scribes, and, finally, they manage to trace a prophecy, Micah 5:2: 'But you, O Bethlehem of Ephrathah, who are one of the little clans of Judah, from you shall come forth for me one who is to rule in Israel, whose origin is from old, from ancient days.' As in the prophecy of the virgin birth, Matthew quotes the Greek text and adapts it slightly, and therefore his version differs minimally from the Hebrew, but the message is the same. The messianic ruler will be born in Bethlehem, a town of David. Again, we must keep in mind that Micah 5:2 was never quoted by Jews who expected the Messiah at this time – the Essenes did not refer to it, and nor did Herod. Only when the astronomers arrived from the observatory of Sippar and asked questions about a saviour-king born in Judah did the scribes eventually find Micah's prophecy and relate it to what had happened in Bethlehem. This town, one of the little villages in Judah, but, as Matthew now emphasizes with pleasure, by no means the least among them, replaced the much more glorious 'City of David', Jerusalem. Matthew did not invent Bethlehem as the birthplace of Jesus. He had no reason to do so, and the analysis of the text and its historical context demonstrates that he gave the facts as he had researched and knew them, accurately and reliably. Those who propagate the myth that Jesus was born in Nazareth are guilty of unscholarly obfuscation.

To end this chapter, let us consider briefly what we know about the qualifications of the Gospel author, Levi-Matthew.

As we have seen, the author of the Gospel has always, from the earliest texts that discuss such questions, been identified with the disciple Levi-Matthew. We know that the name 'Matthew' was attached to the Gospel scroll at a very early stage, while his contemporaries were still alive: the first copies of the Gospels were, of course, published as scrolls, not as 'book-format' codices (these came later). And in antiquity, scrolls were published with a leather or papyrus strip attached to the handle, a so-called *sittybos*, which identified the contents — basically the role played by book spines today. If there was only one book on a given subject, let's say, the history of the Macedonian Wars, the author's name was not always mentioned. But as soon as several works of the same genre or on the same subject were available, the names of the authors were needed to distinguish between the scrolls. In other words, whatever the original order of publication of the four Gospels may have been, as soon as the second one was 'on the market', not only had the author's name to be given on the *sittybos* for the new Gospel but also now retrospectively, for the first Gospel and indeed for all future ones. It means that the four names we still know today were associated with the Gospels within sight of their origins, while people who could confirm, or if necessary contradict and correct the information, were still easily available for comment. Matthew, Mark, Luke and John are anything but the pseudonyms of scribes employed by unknown communities. They were real individuals, known to their contemporaries, who certainly had more information about them than we possess today.

As authors in antiquity did not tend to write about themselves, we are dependent, in most cases, on secondary sources if we want to find out more about them. Even famous, bestselling writers have left us with unanswered questions about their lives. The first name of Tacitus, for example, is uncertain. Was the great historian called Publius Cornelius Tacitus, or did he have a different first name? And who was Velleius Paterculus? A friend of Emperor Tiberius, he wrote a much-neglected Roman history, but our knowledge of his birth, career and the circumstances of his death is sketchy, to say the least. We could go on — the list is long. Matthew, Mark, Luke and John are in good company. But the early commentators, Christian writers of the second and later centuries, have preserved and passed on snippets of data. As far as Matthew is concerned, the identity of disciple and author is a useful starting point. This means we can deduce that his profession was a tax collector: Matthew, who calls himself Matthew, and Luke, who calls him Levi, and Mark, who calls him Levi son of Alphaeus (a not infrequent case of more than one name being used for the same person), agree that he was sitting at his 'tax booth' when Jesus approached him. This was not a tiny hut such as that used by a man looking at passports and checking luggage. The *telônai* — and this is the Greek word used in the Gospels — were tax collectors who worked for the regional rulers or vassal kings and therefore, by implication, for the Roman occupiers. They usually leased a tax office and participated generously in the profits they made. This was a very lucrative job in Capernaum, where sea tax on every catch of fish plus tax levied on those crossing the border between the territories of Galilee, ruled by Herod Antipas, and the Gaulanitis, ruled by Philip, were collected. Levi-Matthew was as rich as he was unpopular, a collaborator who had earned his wealth by helping the rulers to exploit his people. Matthew himself does not make much of it, but Luke tells us that he 'gave a great banquet' for a large crowd when he decided to follow Jesus (Luke 5:29). Small wonder that the Pharisees complained to Jesus, 'Why do you eat with tax collectors and sinners?' and got their put-down: 'Those who are well have no need of a physician, but those who are sick. I have come to call not the righteous, but the sinners to repentance.'

However, not everyone could become a tax collector. Certain qualifications were needed, among them the ability to write shorthand protocols. As we saw in Chapter 2, a first reference to shorthand writing among Jews occurs in the Septuagint, the Greek translation of the Hebrew Bible of the third/second centuries BC. 'My heart overflows with a goodly theme, I address my verses to the king; my tongue is like the pen of a swift scribe', we read in Psalm 45:1. In the Greek text, the swift scribe has become a stenographer. And since it was the purpose of this Greek translation of the Psalms to help Jews who could not read Hebrew any longer to understand the text, it follows that the Greek word *oxygráphos*, stenographer, was one they knew. In the first century BC, Cicero's secretary Tiro invented his own system of Latin shorthand writing, the so-called 'Tironian notes'. At the time of Matthew, shorthand techniques were widespread, but not all of them followed rules still known to us. Thus, many shorthand manuscripts have remained undeciphered. But why was Matthew's knowledge useful to him as a future disciple and Gospel writer? A plausible scenario has been suggested, which takes us back to the real-life circumstances of Jesus and his contemporaries.

Jesus, who had spoken to gatherings from Galilee, the Decapolis, Jerusalem, Judea and from regions beyond the Jordan, saw the crowds and knew of a place where he could speak to them all, up a mountain not far from Capernaum (Matthew 5:1). The mountain has been identified, so to speak, by Christian tradition and is called the 'Mount of the Beatitudes', but the early twentieth-century church on the hillock marks the wrong spot. Up there, the winds tend to blow so noisily that one cannot hear one's own words, let alone those of a person addressing a multitude. Further down the south-west facing slope, towards Tabgha, there is a natural semi-circle, which still looks just like a Greco-Roman theatre. Here, a sizeable crowd could sit and listen while a speaker, standing on the 'podium', could be heard easily even by those sitting in the upper 'stalls'. It is an effect that visitors to the theatre in the Greek city of Epidaurus will be shown by tourist guides, but above Capernaum, it is a natural, not a man-made, phenomenon. Jesus knew how to use these landscape features: in Mark's Gospel, we read about the so-called 'Sermon in the Bay' (Mark 4:1–9 and parallels). He took a boat into the middle of a bay and addressed the crowd on the shore. The bay has been located just north of Capernaum: it forms the orchestra and podium of a theatre, and the shoreline is shaped in a semi-circle, suitable for seating an audience. Acoustic experiments on the lake have indeed demonstrated that a person in a boat does not even have to shout to be understood by people sitting or standing in the 'rows' on shore.

Someone like Levi-Matthew, well-informed and professionally interested in crowd movements near his customs office, could have followed them up the hill. After a while, he would have realized that the speaker's message was new, exciting and controversial. He began to take shorthand notes. Jesus, in turn, noticed the writer in the audience. Eventually, he made enquiries about his identity. A few days later, he passed by his office and invited him to join his group of followers. Having had time to think about the message in his notes, Matthew gladly agreed (Matthew 9:9). Thus, although he was only called after the Sermon on the Mount, we have it in his Gospel, as we have all those other addresses and parables that we do not find, or find only in shorter versions, in the other Gospels. Compare, for example, his eyewitness account of Peter's messianic proclamation in chapter 16:13–28, which is much more detailed than Mark's or Luke's versions. Furthermore, this sequence of events helps us to distinguish between the Sermon on the Mount and the Sermon on the Plain recorded by Luke (6:17 – 7:1). They are not two muddled-up versions of the same event, as some scholars still maintain, but two separate sermons on roughly the same subject matter. Quite apart from the differences in location and content, Levi-Matthew was already one of the disciples by this stage (Luke 5:27). It follows that the Sermon on the Plain was given on a later occasion.

This way of approaching the sources may look unorthodox to readers of New Testament introductions and commentaries. How can one possibly believe that there really was a Sermon on the Mount? Is it not, rather, a deliberate construction by the author or his community committee, put together from various traditions? Obviously, the attempt to make sense of the account as we have it, and to place it within the context of archaeology, topography, professional skills and, in general terms, the real world of the period, combines facts with probabilities and possibilities. But this is how we have to deal with all sources from antiquity. Put simply, we no longer know all of the many facets of everyday life that were so commonplace to contemporary writers and readers, and it must be stated once again that the deficiencies are usually ours rather than those of the ancients. Striving to understand the texts and their background, we have to take them seriously without modern prejudice and accept that, in the ironic words of George Kennedy, ancient writers sometimes meant what they said and occasionally even knew what they were talking about.

4

WHAT WAS JESUS' PLACE IN JEWISH TRADITION?

What in fact was 'Jewish tradition' at the time of Jesus?

Jesus was a Jew. Initially, therefore, his place in Jewish tradition was that of any male Jew. He was circumcised on the eighth day and, after forty days, he was presented at the Temple as a firstborn son. The Gospels, written by Jewish authors, take this for granted and do not go into detail. Only Luke mentions the circumcision in passing (2:21), and the church worked out the date on the basis of the fourth-century decision to celebrate Jesus' birth on the 25 December, so that 1 January was fixed as the major festival of 'The Circumcision of Christ'. Since most people are not in a fit state to celebrate anything after the New Year's Eve festivities, it is seldom observed these days and the squeamish have replaced the circumcision by 'The Naming of Jesus' – which is technically correct in so far as the child was given his name on that day – thereby sidelining the unequivocal Jewishness of the event.

In the Middle Ages and until the nineteenth century, Christian composers wrote incidental music for the occasion, and Jan Dismas Zelenka's mass, 'The Circumcision of our Lord Jesus Christ', composed in 1728 (the year when John Gay wrote *The Beggar's Opera*), remains a remarkable example of the musical ingenuity that was once invested in this most Jewish of inititiation rites, even by Christians. The presentation at the Temple, thirty-two days after the circumcision, was a ritual that had to be abandoned when the Temple was destroyed by the Romans in AD 70. Luke explains the ritual to Theophilus, the dedicatee of his Gospel, and to all other readers as though the Temple was still standing; it is a custom observed by pious Jews to the present day.

The first part of the ritual does not depend on the Temple. A mother is 'unclean' for the seven days before the circumcision. Afterwards, she has to remain at home for another thirty-three days. What follows is a rite that no longer exists, as it had to be observed at the Temple in Jerusalem. On the fortieth day, the mother offered a sacrifice near the so-called Court of Women, at the Nicanor Gate of the Temple: 'Then, after the purification had been completed in accordance with the Law of Moses, they brought him up to Jerusalem to present him to the Lord, as prescribed in the Law of the Lord: "Every firstborn shall be deemed to belong to the Lord," and also to make the offering as stated in the Law: "A pair of turtle doves or two young pigeons".' (Luke 2:22–24). Again, the day is commemorated in the calendar of the church on 2 February. Luke goes on to underline the Jewishness of the occasion. He tells of the two people who address

Mary and Joseph at the Temple. First Simeon, who recognizes Jesus as the messiah and praises God with words that have entered the liturgy of Christian churches as the 'Nunc dimittis' (from the first words in Latin), and are usually said or sung in the traditional version: 'Lord, now lettest thou thy servant depart in peace, according to thy word. For mine eyes have seen thy salvation, which thou hast prepared before the face of all people, to be a light to the Gentiles, and to be the glory of thy people Israel' (Luke 2:29–32). Clearly, and whatever the English translation used to quote it, this is a truly Jewish proclamation to all Jews and to the whole world.

In Luke's account, it is followed by the words of a prophetess, Hanna Bat Phanuel, or, in English, Anna the daughter of Phanuel, 'of the tribe of Asher'. Luke, careful enough to record her place in ancient Jewish tradition, presents her as a voice of devotion and insight into the fulfilment of ancient prophecies. Isaiah 52:9–10 is behind her farsighted exclamation: 'Break forth together into shouts of joy, you ruins of Jerusalem, for the Lord has comforted his people, he has redeemed Jerusalem. The Lord has bared his holy arm in the sight of all nations, and the whole world from end to end shall see the deliverance wrought by our God.' Both statements, Simeon's and Anna's, highlight a message that set the tone for Jesus' future ministry: he was sent as the Messiah of the Jews and, at the same time, as the Jewish Messiah for the whole world. Some thirty years later, when Jesus speaks to a Samaritan woman, someone who was not accepted as Jewish by Jewish officialdom, he accepts her devotion, realizing that she is a true believer, but he insists that 'salvation comes from the Jews' (John 4:22). Anna's prayerful devotion is unmistakable: she 'worshipped night and day with fasting and prayer'. And it is this type of commitment that Jesus recommends to his disciples when they fail to heal a young boy possessed by a demon (Mark 9:29). This kind of demon, he says, cannot be driven out 'except by prayer and fasting'. In such an extreme situation – whether of fervent messianic expectancy, as in Anna's case, or of fighting evil powers – the whole person, mind and body, must be prepared. In Greco-Roman thought, mind and body were separate entities. A devout Jew, however, saw them as an indivisible whole. In one of the many perplexing decisions arrived at by the committee that gave us the standard Greek text of the New Testament according to Nestle-Aland and the United Bible Societies, the fasting was deleted from Mark 9:29, and a non-Jewish Jesus suddenly declares that a particular kind of demon cannot be driven out except by prayer. Practically all recent translations have followed this unjustifiable decision, and readers who do not know what the correct Greek text of Mark's Gospel really says have been led astray (more on this in Chapter 9). It is one example among many that demonstrate that Christians, even Christian New Testament critics, still have to learn from the Jewishness of Jesus. The events surrounding his birth and early years set the tone.

Luke adds one further snippet of information about the early years, and again it serves to emphasize the Jewishness of Jesus. It is the time of the Passover festival; he is twelve years old and Mary and Joseph take him to Jerusalem

(Luke 2:41–52). After the festival, the group of pilgrims that had come from Nazareth returns without noticing that Jesus is missing. Everyone, it seems, assumes that Jesus is with other boys in the party and it is only after a while that they notice his absence. Joseph and Mary return to Jerusalem where they find him in the Temple, debating with teachers of Holy Scripture. So far, there is nothing unusual about the story. In a caravan of many families from Nazareth, those in charge of the children may not have missed little Jesus immediately – who has not read media reports about children left behind by accident even today? And a twelve-year-old discussing the Law of Moses would not have come as a complete surprise, either. At this age, Jesus was approaching Jewish adulthood. The Bar Mitzvah ceremony, celebrated when a boy becomes, literally, a 'Son of the Commandment' on his thirteenth birthday, continues to this day. It is not explicitly mentioned in the Bible but in several medieval sources, where it is described in such a way that an ancient Jewish practice should be presumed. In the years before the ceremony, a boy had to learn how to read from the Hebrew Bible and to learn long passages by heart, particularly from the Torah and the Psalms. There are synagogues today that require five years of religious education before the Bar Mitzvah. This, too, is based on ancient precedent. At twelve years of age, Jesus was therefore close to the end of his 'training' and would have used every opportunity to deepen his understanding of the Law. The reaction of the teachers fits a general scenario too – there are always some pupils who are more gifted than others and whose questions and answers sound remarkably mature. 'And all who heard him were amazed at his intelligence and the answers he gave' (2:47). Luke is at pains to place young Jesus in an everyday Jewish context. This is not to say that he ignores or denies his divine Sonship – his Gospel makes it abundantly clear that Jesus is the Messiah and the Son of God (1:26–38, and so on). But as Christians proclaim in the creeds, Jesus was fully man and fully God, and his childhood and boyhood years serve to uphold the observation that he was fully man, and a Jewish one at that.

Only following this do we find the subtle change from the human to the divine. When Mary asks him how he could do this to her and Joseph, adding, 'Your father and I have been anxiously searching for you,' he reminds her of his pedigree. For while Joseph was his adoptive father and, therefore, in legal terms, as good as his father in the flesh, his divine father had to be given his right. God's house was not in Nazareth but at the Temple in Jerusalem: 'Did you not know that I was bound to be in my Father's house?' Luke adds that 'they did not understand what he had said,' which of course does not mean that they had forgotten the circumstances of his birth. For a moment, they are simply overwhelmed, failing to come to terms with the fact that Jesus, on the eve of adulthood, is about to give preference to his divine father. As human beings, it hurts them, and their reaction is quite understandable. And yet it remains only a brief moment of premonition. Jesus returns home to Nazareth with them and the period before his first public appearance is spent in the community of his family and relatives in Galilee. 'He continued to be under their authority,' Luke writes, and 'his mother treasured up all these things in her heart.' The fourth commandment was honoured, and in later Christian teaching, Paul takes this up in his letter to the Colossians (3:20): 'Children, obey your parents in everything, for that is pleasing to God and is the Christian way.'

The Jewishness of Jesus runs like a thread through the writings of the New Testament. Luke begins by focusing on the early years; the other Gospel authors start with his baptism by the Jewish prophet John the Baptist, who was a close relative; while Paul, for example, hardly ever mentions him without adding the epithet 'Christ', which is Greek for 'Messiah'. In recent scholarly debates, and in the popular media, attempts have been made to link Jesus with the Essenes or the Pharisees, as many of his teachings bear resemblance to Essene and Pharisaic concepts. This does not get us very far, however. If Jesus was the Messiah, if he was seen as such by his followers and by many observers, and if he never contradicted these claims and proclamations (cf. Matthew 16:17), it follows that he would hardly have been acceptable to all as a member or adherent of one single movement among the conflicting Jewish interest groups and lobbies. On the other hand, as Messiah and Son of God, as miracle worker and wandering teacher, he needed to be informed about beliefs and tendencies among his fellow Jews. None of the three big Jewish movements, the Sadducees, Pharisees and Essenes, was a secret sect. They all acted in the open. The Sadducees, who derived their name from Zadok the Priest, formed the Temple priesthood and the majority of the Jewish Council, the Sanhedrin. They acknowledged only the Torah, the five books of Moses, as the absolute yardstick of God's Law and refused to recognize any teachings that they failed to find there, such as the explicit prophecies of a bodily resurrection spelled out in Isaiah, Ezekiel and Daniel. They also refused to acknowledge the oral teaching of the great rabbinical schools of Hillel, Shammai and the others. The Pharisees, on the other hand, had separated themselves from this narrow outlook. Their name, in Hebrew *P'rushim*, means 'the separated ones'. They accepted the whole Tanach, that is, all the books of what Christians call the Old Testament, as normative, and they cherished the oral teaching of the rabbis. After the destruction of the Temple in AD 70, when only they survived from among the great movements, one of their most important acts was to collect these oral teachings in writing, in the Mishnah and, finally, in the two Talmuds, the Talmud Yerushalmi, or Jerusalem Talmud, and the Talmud Bavli, or Babylonian Talmud.

Neither of these two movements should be seen as monolithic. The Sadducees opened their ranks to thousands of auxiliary priests all over the country and this paved the way for more flexible attitudes at the margins. For example, Zechariah, the father of John the Baptist, was one such auxiliary priest (Luke 1:5; 1:8–23). In his song of praise, the so-called 'Benedictus' (Luke 1:68–79), he quoted from Genesis, but also from Isaiah, Jeremiah and Malachi. His son, John the Baptist, later based his whole prophetic ministry on a word not from the Torah, but from Isaiah: 'A voice cries in the wilderness: "Prepare the way for the Lord; clear a straight path for him. Every ravine shall be filled in, and every mountain and hill levelled; winding paths shall be straightened, and rough ways made smooth; and all mankind shall see God's deliverance"' (Isaiah 40:3–5, slightly modified by John the Baptist). The Pharisees mainly followed two schools of thought: one in the footsteps of Hillel and another one, stricter in observance and interpretation, in the footsteps of Shammai. Sha'ul/Paul, who insisted that he remained a Pharisee even as a follower of Jesus (Acts 23:6; Philippians 3:5), was a disciple of Gamaliel the Great who himself belonged to the school of Hillel. Finally, the Essenes, who had split from the Sadducees in the mid-second century BC at the latest, developed their own system of messianic expectancy. Their interpretations of Holy Scripture and their manuals of community discipline were meant to prepare all Jews for the last days, when the priestly messiah from the line of Aaron and the messiah from the line of David would reveal themselves (or himself, if they should turn out to be one and the same). A fierce battle against internal and external enemies would end in the victory of the Prince of the Community, which was their term for the triumphant messiah. Fellow Jews who refused to accept these teachings were cursed in dramatic sequences of rhetoric. In the Essenes' worldview, there were no compromises.

Anyone who thinks that the often harsh criticism of Jewish errors that Jesus, the Gospel authors and Paul express is 'anti-Jewish', if not 'anti-Semitic', should read Essene writings. The inter-Jewish attacks in pages of the New Testament pale by comparison. Sadducees, Pharisees, Essenes and the first Christians, all of them Jews after all, fought for the scriptural high ground. It was an impassioned fight. And Jesus was aware of these spiritual battlefields. Wherever he went, he met and often actively sought out adherents of these Jewish movements. The similarities between his teachings and several of their tenets should not surprise us – after all, they were all Jews who based their proclamation and their practice on common ground, namely the ancient Law of the Torah. Even the Essenes did it. In fact, their name, 'Essenes', which probably means 'the (very) pious ones', occurs in the writings of Philo of Alexandria, Pliny the Elder, Flavius Josephus and some others, but never in their own scrolls. Their name for themselves was 'Yachad' (pronounced with a -ch as in the Scottish word 'loch'), which means 'union' or 'the unified one(s)', and the scrolls make it clear that this was the 'Union under the Torah'. Thus, if everyone adheres to the very same Law of Moses, overlap and similarities are obligatory. The teachings of Jesus and the first Christians are no exception. The differences only become apparent at the next stage: how to interpret and apply these laws for the present and the future, and how far to go in the acceptance of later writings or oral additions.

The Sadducees, as we saw, strictly adhered to the Torah and the Torah only, whereas the Pharisees developed an elaborate system of rabbinic interpretations. The Essenes, too, interpreted the Torah – and the Prophets – according to their needs and expectations, and they introduced a new form of commentary on the biblical books, the 'Pesher' (plural 'Pesharim'). Pesher means 'interpretation', and the word often occurs in the scrolls to signal the beginning of a commentary after a quote from the Bible. Whole books were interpreted in this way, the most famous example being the 'Habakkuk Pesher' from Qumran Cave I, which has survived not as tiny snippets, as many other Qumran writings have, but in the form of a fragmentary scroll. Chapters 1:1 – 2:20 are quoted and individually commented on, one by one, in thirteen columns. But the Pesharim were no ordinary Bible commentaries. The Essene commentators were not interested in a strictly historical or critical analysis; they were looking for the eternal, eschatological meaning of the verses. Thus, the quoted verse may have been changed, or rather adapted, to the theology of the community, to get at the deeper meaning of the prophetic voice. Jesus was aware of this technique and applied it to his oral teaching. The early Christians used it in their writings.

In his Sermon on the Mount, for example, Jesus quoted the prohibition of murder from the Ten Commandments and interpreted it for his messianic community: 'You have heard that it was said to those of ancient times, "You shall not murder," and "whoever murders shall be liable to judgment." But I say to you that if you are angry with a brother, you will be liable to judgment; and if you insult a brother, you will be liable to the council, and if you say, "You fool," you will be liable to the hell of fire' (Matthew 5:21–22). Jesus tightened the ancient Law, which would be politically incorrect today, when laws and their implementation tend to be softer, but in doing so, he would have found favour with the Essenes, and also, as an uncompromising oral teacher and interpreter of the Law, with the the stricter wing of the Pharisees. He did not interpret the Torah so as to please the leading Jewish movements, though. On other occasions, when the Ten Commandments were not at stake, he advocated a down-to-earth approach, which was bound to alienate the

Essenes and the Shammai school of the Pharisees. This was particularly apparent in his teaching about Sabbath observance (Matthew 12:1–14). Plucking heads of grain and eating them on the Sabbath was anathema to the stricter Pharisees, as was the healing of a man who had a withered hand. Jesus taught that 'it is lawful to do good on the Sabbath' and that 'the Sabbath was made for man, and not man for the Sabbath' (Mark 2:27). The Gospels agree that the opponents among the Pharisees found these actions and teachings so destructive to their orthodoxy that they began to 'conspire how to destroy him' and found allies among the 'Herodians', a general term for another group of Jews that probably included the Essenes, who were strongly favoured by Herod the Great and his sons. In the so-called 'Damascus Document', their oldest scroll of community regulations and messianic theology, the Essenes certainly regarded the plucking and eating of fruit in the field on the Sabbath as a punishable offence, and when Jesus said that a sheep that has fallen into a pit should be rescued even on the Sabbath (Matthew 12:11), he directly opposed an Essene ruling.

Breaking the Sabbath could be punished by stoning the offender to death (Numbers 15:32–35). The Essenes generally preferred to impose a seven-year prison sentence. It is noteworthy, though, that not all of them appear to have become and remained opponents of Jesus. According to many scholars, Acts 6:7 refers to Essene priests at their outpost on the south-western hill – today's Mount Zion – in Jerusalem, who became Christians after Easter: 'The word of God continued to spread; the number of the disciples increased greatly in Jerusalem, and a great many of the priests became obedient to the faith.' As for the Pharisees, not all of them adhered to the lethal interpretation of the Sabbath laws, and many would have agreed with Jesus. Nicodemus was certainly one of those pro-Jesus Pharisees (John 7:45–51; 19:39). The Gospels do not attack the whole Pharisaic movement, nor all of the Essenes or Sadducees as enemies of Jesus. The controversies always concern those of their members whom Jesus regarded as error-bound, hypocrites and false teachers. There is no trace anywhere in his words and in the Gospel accounts of an all-out attack against them, nor can it be shown that all of them hated Jesus and conspired against him. These were indeed heated inter-Jewish debates, and then, as today, Sabbath observance was one of the areas that concerned every single Jew. The later Pharisees who compiled the Talmud in the centuries after the destruction of the Temple agreed with Jesus' interpretation: helping the sick and saving lives is mandatory even on the Sabbath. According to the Babylonian Talmud, Rabbi Jonathan, the son of Joseph, taught that 'the Sabbath is given into your hands, it is not you who are given into the hands of the Sabbath' (Babylonian Talmud, 'Yoma' 84 b, 85 b). This is a form of rhetorical figure called 'antithetic parallelism', and rabbis still use it today. In his Yom Kippur message of September 2004, the Israeli Chief Rabbi, Jona Metzger, said that those ultraorthodox Jews who incite other Jews to fratricidal war over the planned withdrawal of settlements from the Gaza Strip should think again: 'Those pious Jews are careful that only things that are *kosher* go into their mouths, but they should also be careful that only words that are *kosher* will come out of their mouths.' Rabbi Jesus had taught something very similar almost two thousand years before Rabbi Jona (Matthew 15:11): 'It is not what goes into the mouth that defiles a person, but it is what comes out of the mouth that defiles.'

The death and resurrection of Jesus was a challenge to mainstream Judaism. Caiaphas, the high priest, and Pontius Pilate, the Roman prefect, were figures of derision and hate. In fact, the Babylonian Talmud later put a threefold 'Woe' on Caiaphas and his family. But regardless of the moral and ethical deficiencies of those who collaborated to get Jesus out of the way, the fact remained that he was crucified. This meant that the curse of Deuteronomy 21:22–23 applied: 'When someone is convicted of a crime punishable by death and is executed, and you hang him on a tree, his corpse must not remain all night upon the tree; you shall bury him that same day, for anyone hung on a tree is under God's curse.' Could the true Messiah be crucified? The simple answer, of course, is no. In those days, the vast majority of Jews expected a victorious messiah, not a suffering and crucified one. No one, not even the disciples, immediately thought of the prophecy in Isaiah 53:8–9: 'By a perversion of justice he was taken away. Who could have imagined his future? For he was cut off from the land of the living, stricken for the transgression of my people. They made his grave with the wicked and his tomb with the rich, although he had done no violence, and there was no deceit in his mouth.' Nor was it at the forefront of their minds to understand Isaiah 53:5 when they saw Jesus on the cross: 'He was wounded for our transgressions, crushed for our iniquities; upon him was the punishment that made us whole, and by his bruises we are healed.' It is never easy to change one's mind; many of the opponents simply refused to accept the miracle of the resurrection by claiming that the disciples had stolen the body (Matthew 27:62–66; 28:11–15), certainly one of the more ridiculous subterfuges in human history. On the other hand, many opponents and doubters (including his own brother James, the disciple Thomas and, eventually, Paul) were convinced by what they saw and experienced, and, as the book of Acts reliably informs us, thousands of Jews became Christians in the week after Easter Day. In other words, it was anything but impossible for devout Jews to accept the crucified and risen Jesus as Messiah and saviour.

Still today, there is a growing number of Messianic Jews: Jews who believe in Jesus without necessarily joining a Christian church. In Jerusalem, for example, the Anglican 'Christ Church' near Jaffa Gate gives them shelter and allows them to celebrate their services in Hebrew without expecting them to become Anglicans. These Messianic Jews realize full well that orthodox Judaism raises numerous objections against Jesus; in some circles, his Hebrew name Yeshua may not even be pronounced. Some of these questions must be addressed in open-minded debate. How, for example, can there be a Eucharist or Holy Communion where Christians eat the body and drink the blood of Christ, if the consumption of any form of blood (not to mention cannibalism) is strictly ruled out by Jewish Law? Where is the worldwide peace, traditionally associated with the arrival of the Messiah? Here we come full circle. The Jews who passed on the message of the Jew

Jesus not only saw these problems but they addressed them, as Jews, in their writings. It was obvious to them that messianic peace was not human political peace, and that Holy Communion, celebrating the real presence of Christ, was neither cannibalism nor an infringement of the dietary laws of observant Jews. Interpreting the Law was never a one-way street; the Essenes, the Pharisees and the first Christians, with everything they had in common, agreed to differ in many respects. Whichever way we may tend to lean in our own assessment, we should never forget that Jesus himself, the disciples and the authors of the New Testament writings were Jews, remained Jews and never dreamed of betraying Judaism. Jesus and the origins of Christianity are Jewish — dare we deny this fact of history?

5

DID JESUS REALLY DO MIRACLES?

There are miracles all around us, even today. We may not always be precise when we use the word, but we are certainly generous in its use. 'It's a miracle!' Who has not heard these words, even in the most mundane circumstances? Accordingly, the *BBC English Dictionary* defines a miracle first as 'a surprising and fortunate event, discovery or invention', and gives two examples: 'his policies created the climate for the economic miracle' and 'the miracle of modern communications'. Only the second definition, 'also a wonderful and surprising event that is believed to be caused by God', comes close to the original meaning, with this example: 'millions of pilgrims want to believe in the miracle'. It is an odd definition, leaving Jesus the miracle worker out of the picture and somehow omitting the fact that a miracle is first of all an act, not an event. When we talk about the miracles performed by Jesus, we mean something he did, like healing Peter's mother-in-law, or turning water into wine, to name but two of his earliest miracles. The New Testament does not state that Christians will lose the ability to perform them with the end of the book of Acts. When Paul writes about the gifts of the Spirit, the gifts of healing and the working of miracles are expressly mentioned among them (I Corinthians 12:9–10). The Roman Catholic Church demands a thorough process of medical analysis at Lourdes, for example, before miracles will be acknowledged. The possibility of illusions, even of downright satanic manipulation, has to be borne in mind. Paul already warned against this danger in his second letter to the Thessalonians (2:9–12). You cannot even become a saint if there have not been at least two attested miracles performed by you in some way or other. Are miracles then all figments of the imagination?

Let us play with numbers for a moment. By the autumn of 2002, Pope John Paul II had canonized four hundred and fifty saints. This means, statistically, there must have been at least nine hundred medically attested healing miracles and some other miracles to boot. By comparison, there are 'merely' thirty-four miracles attributed to Jesus. In other words, the popular claim that people in allegedly pre-enlightened Bible times were easily taken in by what they saw and described it as a miraculous act or event is not borne out by sober statistics. Many Bible scholars, however, persist in telling us that the miracles of Jesus are all suspect, some perhaps less so than others (he may have performed the odd healing, after all, when a person was not really sick) and that we should not accept them as historical events in our modern age of space travel and state-of-the-art textual criticism. But what did Jesus really do? And how were his deeds perceived by eyewitnesses? To answer these questions, let us return to the real world of the first century. For this non-Jewish world of Greco-Roman culture, and of all the other civilizations that were known to people in the Holy Land, thanks to international travel and commerce, was confronted with the worldview of the Jews and their certainty that God continued to act among them.

To begin with, we have to understand two surprising facts about the time of Jesus. Miracles were the exception, not the rule. First, it is plainly untrue that Jesus was just one of many so-called miracle workers of his time. And secondly, not one of his contemporaries doubted that he performed his miracles. Even an opponent like the high priest Caiaphas saw some of them with his own eyes (Matthew 21:14–17) and accepted others at face value. He realized that they were messianic and eventually took action against Jesus precisely because a messiah was the last person he needed in his power-conscious, highly sensitive dealings with the Romans and their prefect, Pontius Pilate. The first of these two facts is perhaps the more surprising one. The Old Testament is full of miraculous acts. In the Torah, the book of Exodus could be called a story of God's continuing miracle with his people. The word itself occurs again and again, and the theme is set in Exodus 3:19–20: 'I know that the Pharaoh will not let you go unless compelled by a mighty hand. So I will stretch out my hand and strike Egypt with all the miracles which I will perform in it. Then he will let you go.' God's covenant with his people comprises 'miracles such as have not been performed in all the earth or in any nation' (Exodus 34:10–11). And God uses Moses as his vehicle: 'And the Lord said to Moses, "When you go back to Egypt, see that you perform before Pharaoh all the miracles that I have put in your power"' (Exodus 4:21). Aaron, too, is invested with these powers (Exodus 11:10). In Deuteronomy, the final book of the Torah, God's mighty presence during his people's exodus is confirmed: 'The Lord brought us out of Egypt with a mighty hand and an outstretched arm, with a terrifying display of power, and with signs and miracles' (26:8) – and it is this verse that is quoted by Stephen, the first martyr of the Jerusalem Church, as an example of the God of glory revealing himself in miracles (Acts 7:36).

Moses and his brother Aaron have remained outstanding models throughout Jewish history – Moses as the archetypal leader and author of the Torah, Aaron as the first of all priests. Jesus himself, a descendant of Aaron on his mother's side, regarded and quoted Moses as the authoritative voice of Judaism. Small wonder then that the third of the great miracle workers of classical Judaism, Elijah (1 Kings 17:8–24, etc.), was treated in a similar vein. God promised that he would send Elijah 'before the great and terrible day of the Lord comes' (Malachi 4:5), and Jesus taught that John the Baptist was Elijah returned (Matthew 11:14). On the high Mount of the Transfiguration, Moses and Elijah appear to Jesus and are seen by Peter, James and John (Matthew 17:1–13).

Awe-inspiring as this is, the Old Testament writings do not devalue the miraculous by presenting an uninterrupted stream of miracles and miracle-workers. On the contrary, actual miracles are sparse. God and his prophets do not have to 'perform' all the time to be or remain credible. Thus, while many New Testament introductions and theologies continue to state that Jesus was one of many, if not countless, miracle-workers, we should not be surprised that only three people were regarded as performers of miracles in the first centuries BC and AD. Honi ha-Me'aggel ('the Circle-Drawer') and Hanina ben Dosa were Jews, but neither of these was a contemporary rival of Jesus. The third was Apollonius of Tyana, a Greek wandering teacher from Tyana, a town in Cappadocia, today in central Turkey. He was born at the beginning of the first century AD and died towards its end. His alleged deeds and sayings have survived thanks to a historical novel by Philostratus, written in about AD 220. If and to what extent they may be authentic remains an open question. It is certain that Philostratus, unlike the Gospel authors who wrote about Jesus, had no direct access to eyewitness material, nor was he an eyewitness himself. The miracles ascribed to Apollonius are shrouded in secret, for he was convinced that ordinary people were not supposed to hear or understand his 'magic' formulas. They even include elements of cruelty, like the stoning to death of a beggar to drive out the plague from the city of Ephesus. Philostratus wrote for the Empress Julia Domna. He and the empress were clearly motivated by anti-Christian interests. Therefore, as a historical resource about a contemporary miracle worker of Jesus, the novel is useless. However, it does provide us with a glimpse into the pagan world of myths that Jesus and his followers had opposed relentlessly almost two hundred years before Philostratus put pen to paper.

The other two, like Jesus, were both Jews. Honi the Circle-Drawer lived in the first century BC. Only one miracle is attributed to him. By prayer and a bit of attempted blackmail, he persuaded God, addressing him from within a circle, to let it rain on the scorched soil. It did indeed rain, but not enough. Honi prayed again, but this time there was too much rain. So he prayed again and now there was just the right amount. He prayed a fourth time, and the rain stopped. In the Babylonian Talmud ('Taanit' 23a), the story is told with a good measure of humour, but the question was asked if Honi had not 'harassed God with his persistent requests'. It would be absurd to take Honi seriously as a rival to Jesus in the field of prophetic and messianic miracles.

Hanina ben Dosa was of a different calibre. He began his public ministry some twenty years after the death of Jesus. Six miracles are attributed to him – certainly more than Honi, but, given the fact that, unlike Jesus, he was not killed at the zenith of his career, it is a somewhat meagre harvest. None of his miracles is messianic in any sense of the word. They concern the healing of people suffering from a high temperature, or, in one case, Hanina's own survival from a serpent's bite. The Talmud, compiled three to five centuries after Hanina, tells these stories with a sense of admiration. From its perspective, Hanina stood out as a singular figure in the first century AD, since Jesus was not recognized by the Talmudic compilers. A lesson is taught by each of Hanina's miracles. It is this 'didactic' aspect that links Hanina with Jesus after all and separates them both from Apollonius of Tyana. But here the parallel between these two Jewish miracle workers ends. In brief, at that time, Jesus was clearly in a league of his own. The notion that Jesus was just one of many must be relegated to the scrapheap of myths about New Testament times.

If anyone came remotely close to Jesus, it was of course his own disciples and apostles, to whom he himself had given the power to heal, restore life and drive out demons. It became a hallmark of the community in Jerusalem: 'More than ever, believers were added to the Lord, great numbers of both men and women, so that they even carried out the sick into the streets, and laid them on cots and mats, in order that Peter's shadow might fall on some of them as he came by. A great number of people would also gather from the towns around Jerusalem, bringing the sick and those tormented by unclean spirits, and they were all cured' (Acts 5:14–16; see also Acts 2:43; 3:1–16; 9:32–42; 19:11–20; 20:7–12; Romans 15:18–19, etc.). Peter and Paul certainly surpassed Hanina. A particularly striking event, where the Jewish world of the apostles and the pagan world of gods clashed, took place at Lystra in Lycaonia (now southern Turkey). Paul healed a man with crippled feet, and 'when the crowds saw what Paul had done, they shouted in the Lycaonian language, "The gods have come to us in human form!" Barnabas they called Zeus, and Paul they called Hermes, because he was the chief speaker. The priest of Zeus, whose temple was just outside the city, brought oxen and garlands to the gates; he and the crowds wanted to offer sacrifice' (Acts 14:8–18). Needless to say, Barnabas and Paul protested and admonished them 'to turn from these worthless things to the living God' but 'they scarcely restrained the crowds from offering sacrifice to them'.

We may ask how often the people at Lystra had seen comparable miracles if they went over the top like this in their ritual jubilation. Healing miracles were anything but frequent, be it in pagan or Jewish society. When Jesus healed a paralytic, the witnesses in Capernaum 'glorified God, saying: "We have never seen anything like this!"' (Mark 2:12). When he healed a mute demoniac, 'the crowds were amazed and said: "Never has anything like this been seen in Israel"' (Matthew 9:33). And when he healed a man born blind, the man himself exclaimed: 'Never since the world began has it been heard that anyone opened the eyes of a person born blind' (John 9:32).

No one disputed these healings. Occasionally, Jesus' enemies merely tried to deny that God was acting through him or that he acted in his own divine power: 'By the ruler of the demons [that is, the devil], he casts out demons' (Matthew 9:34). In AD 178, one of the fiercest critics of nascent Christianity, a certain Celsus (Kelsos in Greek), a man who disputed the validity of the Christian message with every philosophical and pseudo-rational argument he could muster, never for a moment doubted the historicity of Jesus' miracles. They had all happened – but, Celsus alleged, Jesus had learned the art of miraculous healings and other such deeds when he stayed in Egypt as a young boy and was taught by Egyptian magicians. If this was so, it remains to be asked why Egyptian magicians themselves never performed such miracles. But in passing, the historian notices something else: Celsus, the anti-Christian critic, also accepted the historicity of the flight into Egypt, and that is something quite a few Christian New Testament critics have abandoned, albeit for spurious reasons.

Thus, acknowledging the veracity of Jesus' and the apostles' miracles and accepting them as signs of the one and only God acting in human history were not necessarily one and the same thing in those days. At Lystra, Paul and Barnabas were hailed as gods personified because such acts and events were associated with gods or their holy places, such as the shrine of Asclepius in Epidaurus. Yet even at a shrine dedicated to the Greco-Roman godhead of healing, miracles did not happen all that frequently. The travelling writer Pausanias visited the shrine in the mid-second century AD, and instead of a continuous track record of healing miracles, all he found were six inscriptions with healings dating back to the fourth century BC; three of them and the fragment of another have been discovered by archaeologists. Most of those who came to the temple of Asclepius or to the priests at any other temple left unhealed; conversely, not a single person who turned in faith to the historical Jesus and his apostles was disappointed. The uniqueness of Jesus' ministry and message was all the more obvious to the Jews and Gentiles of his day, irrespective of their varying attempts to explain how it had been brought about.

If we want to do justice to the miracles of Jesus, there is something else we should take into consideration. Rather than looking at each of the thirty-four miracles in detail and placing them in scholarly categories, let us see how Jesus himself used them to help people understand who he was. There is one incident in the Gospels that provides the evidence in a nutshell. It was briefly described in Chapter 2; let us now look at it in some detail.

Jesus is approached by the disciples of John the Baptist.

John is imprisoned by Herod Antipas, in the fortress of Machaerus, east of the Dead Sea. He knows he is going to die. And, understandably, he wants to find out if Jesus really is 'the one who is to come', the prophesied Anointed One of God – in Hebrew, the 'Messiah', in Greek, the 'Christ'. After all, John himself had spoken as the voice of one crying in the wilderness, proclaiming none other than Jesus. But John knows that none of the majestic deeds he had associated with Jesus as the messiah (baptizing with the Holy Spirit and fire, burning the chaff with unquenchable fire) have happened by this stage. In all likelihood, he would not live long enough to see them happen. Is there anything Jesus can do to convince him that he, John, has been right after all? Does Jesus send John's messengers back with some soothing generalities? Does he reiterate the ancient Jewish prophecies that John himself had referred to in the first place? He does nothing of the sort. Instead, he replies with a list of miracles he had performed, which many of John's disciples who were now present had witnessed. This is his list as we find it in Matthew 11:4–6 and Luke 7:22–23, alongside the occasions on which Jesus had performed them:

> The blind receive their sight (already fulfilled in Matthew 9:27–30)
>
> The lame walk (fulfilled in Matthew 8:5–13;9:2–7)
>
> The lepers are cleansed (Matthew 8:2–3)
>
> The deaf hear (included in Matthew 4:23 and 9:35; later directly in Mark 7:31–37)

The dead are raised (Matthew 9:18–25)

The poor have good news brought to them
(Matthew 5:3)

This list consists of five miracles and one non-miraculous sign – the good news being brought to the poor, an event which, like the five kinds of miracles, had always been associated with times of salvation and in particular with the Messiah, at least since the prophet Isaiah (see, for example, Isaiah 26:19; 29:18–20; 35:4–6). And these miracles were an integral part of messianic hope at the time of Jesus. As we already know from Chapter 2, a fragment among the Dead Sea Scrolls found in Qumran 4Q 521, underlines these hopes and expectations, which were shared by many Jews. Here is the text:

> The Lord will seek the pious and call the righteous
> by name. Over the humble his spirit will hover and will
> renew the faithful in his strength. And he will honour the
> pious on the throne of his eternal kingdom. He will set
> prisoners free, opening the eyes of the blind, raising up
> those who are bowed down... He shall heal the wounded.
> He shall revive the dead, and bring good news to the poor.

Let us emphasize it once again: the one miracle that was completely new, the healing of the lepers, Jesus places in the middle of his list. There are two groups of two – the blind and the lame, the deaf and the dead – and between them Jesus puts the outcasts and the lepers. In other words, the one miracle no one had expected the Messiah to perform and no one had ever performed before Jesus – the touching and healing of a leper – becomes the centrepiece of his messianic identity. In the society of Jesus Christ, those despised and rejected by everyone else are given pride of place. It is a revolution, an unheard-of redefinition of the social world.

What is more, Jesus does not trumpet this messianic revolution to the world. His miracles are no public showpieces. He does not even look for opportunities to perform them, since he does not want them to be understood as an end in themselves (John 4:48). More than once, he bids the healed to tell no one what had happened. His messiahship is to be revealed and understood in a step-by-step process, which will culminate in Jerusalem. John the Baptist deserves an answer because he will not live to see the miracle of Easter. But for the others, the evidence of the miracles is not meant to be celebrated in the shape of well-staged publicity stunts. Even those miracles where large numbers of people are the recipients – the feeding of the five thousand and of the four thousand – are anything but advertised festivals planned to overwhelm the sceptics.

The miracles of Jesus are a part of his ministry but they do not shape it. They were witnessed, accepted and reported by believers and unbelievers alike. Whether we like it or not, there is no yardstick by which they could be dismissed as legendary. The historian who studies ancient sources has no problem in seeing them as real events. To put it bluntly, the undeniable fact that many if not most of them surpass our human knowledge and experience must not influence our assessment of their historicity. Let us assume for a moment that the Gospels were written as late as many theologians still think. Oral tradition about the miracles of Jesus was available practically everywhere. Contemporary sceptics would have been able to find out if these reports were true or false. We know from a contemporary source that some of those healed by Jesus lived to tell their stories into the early second century. In AD 125, Quadratus, a pupil of the apostles, sent a petition to Emperor Hadrian, defending the Christians and their message. Fragments of this document have been preserved by Eusebius in his *Church History* (4:2, 3). Among other things, Quadratus wrote: 'The deeds of our Saviour were always present, for they were true. Those who were healed, those who rose from the dead: people had not only witnessed how they were healed and rose, but how they were constantly present. Not only while the Saviour was living, but also after he had departed, they lived for some time, so that some of them survived even until our own time.' Again, the message is clear: ask the eyewitnesses, ask those who were healed. A Christian faith built upon incredible accounts, told and written down by unreliable myth-makers, against a critical, well-informed majority? That scenario is just not credible.

6

DID JESUS REALLY DIE
ON THE CROSS?

The death of Jesus on a Roman cross is one of the best
attested events in ancient history. In fact, there is an old
joke among historians about the weird world of some Bible
critics: we know that Jesus was crucified, but was he ever
born? Even so, the legends about his survival and later
endeavours appear to be bestselling material – Dan
Brown's book, *The Da Vinci Code*, has been celebrated as the
most successful hardcover novel ever published. Its
ideological starting point is this: Jesus survived his death
(no resurrection needed here), married Mary Magdalene
and established a dynasty in France. Leonardo da Vinci,
allegedly in the know, therefore placed Mary next to Jesus,
in place of the beloved disciple, in his famous depiction of
the Last Supper. Any historian worth his or her salt will
tell you that if you believe this, you will believe anything.
But why are millions of people willing to be taken in by
Brown and his predecessors, Michael Baigent, Richard
Leigh and Harry Lincoln?

Dan Brown has written a novel and no one expects a novel to be a historically accurate description of past or present events. Unfortunately, though, Brown claims that his book is based on serious research and the documents cited are rendered accurately and truthfully. This sounds impressive, but should not necessarily be taken at face value. When Hitler's diaries were published many years ago and renowned scholars like Hugh Trevor-Roper pronounced them to be authentic, they were quoted, photographed and reproduced in facsimile as accurately as modern techniques allow, and yet they nonetheless turned out to be abysmal forgeries. However, the real problem with *The Da Vinci Code* should be seen in the claims Brown makes about documents that do exist and are undoubtedly not forged: the Gospels, the Nag Hammadi Codices, the Dead Sea Scrolls and others.

Jesus survived the crucifixion, married Mary Magdalene, had a child with her and established a dynasty whose successors are alive and kicking in present-day France. If this sounds familiar, one only has to turn to a worldwide bestseller from the 1980s to find a similar tale, The Holy Blood and the Holy Grail by Michael Baigent, Richard Leigh and Harry Lincoln. It is all there, in all its mind-boggling naffness. But Brown adds a mystery cult of his own: the Holy Grail is not a chalice but the womb of Mary Magdalene, the womb that carried the bloodline of Christ.

Obviously, to anyone who creates such myths and legends, the Gospels are a hindrance. Baigent, Leigh, Lincoln and their imitator Brown have to distort, manipulate and generally explain away what the Gospels say. In his novel, Dan Brown claims that Constantine the Great, the first Christian Roman emperor, destroyed thousands of original manuscripts that told the story of a merely human, far from immortal Jesus. And what evidence does Brown provide? Unsurprisingly, there is nothing remotely suspect anywhere in the sources. By the time of Constantine, in the first half of the fourth century, Gospel manuscripts had reached every corner of the Roman empire, and the emperor would not have been able to destroy them, even if he had tried. Some one hundred pre-Constantinian papyri have survived in more than twenty libraries, from Jerusalem to Cairo, from Oxford to Cambridge, from Berlin to Ann Arbor, from Dublin to Cologne, and in none of them is there any trace of editorial changes. As we saw in a previous chapter, and as a classical philologist from Berlin's prestigious Humboldt University, Dr Ulrich Victor, recently confirmed, ordinary human scribal errors apart, we have the Gospels as they were written; they are early historical records in the mould of Hellenistic historiography.

As always in such books, the Vatican is presented as the evil power, trying to prevent access to the truth. We already have this in another Baigent/Leigh 'classic', *The Dead Sea Scrolls Deception*. It is conveniently ignored that the Vatican did not have access to the scrolls in the decisive years after their discovery. Not a single Vatican scholar ever joined the editorial teams when the scrolls were collected, photographed and handed over to scholars for the painstakingly difficult process of deciphering, transcribing and publishing. The Hebrew and Aramaic scrolls from the Qumran caves do not mention Jesus at all. The American

Robert Eisenman, who was once renowned as an energetic scholar and decipherer, reinterpreted some of them as secret, hidden messages about Jesus, Paul, James and the early church and did not stop doing so even when he was told that these scrolls were written in the first and second centuries BC, before Jesus had even been born. Radiocarbon dating and the paleographical analysis of the handwriting were conclusive, but Eisenman reacted like the German philosopher Hegel who, when told by a student that his theories were contradicted by the facts, simply replied: 'So much the worse for the facts.' The bestselling *The Dead Sea Scrolls Deception* was based on Eisenman's theories.

Another Dead Sea Scrolls scholar, Barbara Thiering, once noted for interesting contributions to serious scholarship, became similarly affected by the Dead Sea Scrolls syndrome (which would appear to be a variant virus of the 'Jerusalem syndrome', which affects people during stays in Jerusalem and causes them to claim that they are King David or Jesus himself). She went a step further and wrote a book, *Jesus the Man*, which claimed that Jesus had married Mary Magdalene on 23 September AD 30 at En Fekhsha, which happens to be the oasis just south of Qumran at the Dead Sea. A daughter was born, but before they could try to produce a son, Jesus was crucified – on 2 February 33, easily the most far-fetched among the many improbable dates that have been suggested instead of the historically realistic 7 April AD 30. No matter – in Thiering's book Jesus did not die anyway but survived a mock crucifixion in a cave at Qumran in the presence of Pontius Pilate, thanks to a magic potion. Jesus fled to Rome, where he died in AD 64, not without having solemnized his marriage to Mary Magdalene once more. According to Thiering, two sons were born, in AD 37 and 44, but then Mary asked for a divorce and left Jesus. Not to be outdone, Jesus married Lydia, the dealer in purple cloth whom Paul had met in Philippi. These fantasies are all the weirder as Thiering did not reject the Gospels, as Dan Brown does in his *Da Vinci Code*, but maintained that all of this can be found in the pages of the New Testament and in the Dead Sea Scrolls – particularly in the Damascus Document – provided one knows how to apply Thiering's own method of 'deciphering' the text. In other words, as Shakespeare might have put it, it is madness with a method.

One could easily go on and present many more flights of fancy. Just one more example: Jesus, the survivor of his crucifixion, returned to India, where he had been to study as a young man, and was buried in the town of Srinagar. This is pure fiction, which has been around ever since a certain Nicolay A. Notovitch first presented it at the end of the nineteenth century, and it has been rehashed in many variations without gaining in plausibility on the way. It is obvious enough that all of these theories are far removed from serious scholarship. They are based on a simple ideology: the New Testament, as the basic collection of documents on which the Christian churches are founded, must be discredited so that the churches themselves will fall. The Roman Catholic Church may always have been the main target of this ideology, but the other churches have no reason to watch idly from the sidelines. It is the general position of Christianity, not of just one church, that Jesus, the Messiah, was the Son of God, that he and only he is the way of truth and freedom, that he and only he died on the cross for the sins of humankind. Idealists and ideologists who imagine a world of equal religions, equal in their claims to embody ways of salvation, peace and closeness to God, must therefore dispute, deny and fight the uniqueness of the Christian faith and its written records. It really is as simple as that. The enemies of Christianity have no choice — other than to return to the sources, of course; and conversely, the defenders of Christianity have no choice, either. There simply is no compromise.

This does not mean, however, that Christians who accept the veracity of their faith will have to block every form of interreligious communication. The dialogue between world religions is more necessary than ever. But how can there be a fruitful dialogue if one of the participants begins by saying that one's own sources are playthings of the changing fashions of theology, prone to be misunderstood by anyone who dares to take them literally, and that they are, in a manner of speaking, open to negotiation? In such a context, popular books that deny or distort the Gospel evidence are merely riding the crest of a wave. Brown, Baigent, Leigh and Thiering may represent the madder fringe of anti-Christian theorizing, but below the surface of the waves, there are institutions like the so-called 'Jesus Seminar' in the States, whose members cast votes on the degree of authenticity of Jesus' sayings and who think that the late and spurious 'Gospel of Peter' or the 'Gospel of Thomas', which omits the suffering and the crucifixion of Jesus, are older and more reliable than the four historical Gospels in the New Testament. One could laugh this off, and perhaps one should, but these people, many of them university professors, find a following and are set on a course to destroy Christianity from within. If Dan Brown tells millions of readers that they should trust the 'Gospel of Thomas', a late collection of sayings that cannot possibly contain historical narratives about Jesus by any stretch of the imagination, he represents the lowest common denominator of positions that have been made palatable by theological seminars and movements.

A retired professor of Divinity at Oxford University recently suggested, apparently in earnest, that people should choose their religion on the basis of their culture. If this was true, the proclamation of Christianity would have no place in the modern world, and Christian mission – commanded by Jesus himself, not once but twice, at the end of Matthew's Gospel and at the beginning of Luke's Acts of the Apostles – would be rendered illegitimate. Furthermore, there is at present no living culture that is based on the insight that the most cruel of ancient Rome's death penalties, the death on the cross, means life for humankind, and that a unique event in world history, the resurrection of a crucified man, confirms and seals this. Western culture has largely abandoned this cornerstone of its existence, or, to put it differently, it is no longer aware of it. When the preamble to the European Constitution was ratified in 2004, it was decided to avoid all reference to God, let alone to Jesus and Christianity, as one of the undeniable roots of Europe. And one of the reasons for this neglect is the ongoing belittling of our history, of the sources and their unequivocal meaning. Likewise, it is no longer politically correct to insist on the death of Jesus on the cross and his resurrection as events in history on one level, and as divine truth on another – for saying so will turn you into a fundamentalist. Professional historians, however, are fundamentalists by definition, as they have to get down to the fundamentals, without ideological or cultural presuppositions. And that is why the historical pursuit of past events is so much more rewarding than the entirely fictitious and novelistic idea that Jesus never died on the cross.

So let us ask again, is there any solid reason to doubt the historicity of the crucifixion and death of Jesus? The twenty-seven writings of the New Testament presuppose it, four of them – the Gospels – describe it and several non-Christian authors concur. In the first century, the most interesting testimony is that of a Jewish-Christian historian, Flavius Josephus. In the early second century, he is joined by the most famous of all Roman historians, Tacitus. In his *Annals* 15:44, he mentions the Christians as victims of Nero's persecution after the fire of Rome in AD 64 and explains that their name is derived from 'Christ (*Christus*, in Latin), who was executed under Tiberius by the procurator Pontius Pilate'. Tacitus does not like Christianity – he calls it a pernicious superstition – but he does not like Nero, either. It is certainly noteworthy that, though Tacitus was an outspoken enemy of the Jews, he does not blame them for the death of Jesus. The man responsible was Pilate, who served under Tiberius. Two centuries later, the first Roman emperor who became a Christian, Constantine the Great, convened the Council of

Nicea in AD 325 and helped to shape the Nicene Creed. Again, we read that Jesus suffered, was crucified and died 'under Pontius Pilate'. Neither Caiaphas nor the Sanhedrin are mentioned anywhere, in none of the several versions of the creed that came into being during the fourth century. They all agree with Tacitus that Jesus was executed — which means that he was certified dead — and that the sole responsibility lay with the Romans. Thus, apart from the historical confirmation of his death on the cross, the Roman sources also underline that Jesus the Jew was not the victim of the Jews.

In passing, perhaps, but not without emphasis, we should note that the *Annals* of Tacitus along with the creeds provide an early antidote to Christian anti-Semitism. When Melito, the Bishop of Sardes, in his Easter homily of about AD 140, called the Jews murderers of God, he initiated a form of hatred of the Jews that permeated the development of Christianity. Melito, it seems, had not read Tacitus. The creeds, all of them, should be understood as an attempt, two centuries after Melito, to correct the increasingly widespread tendency to blame the Jews. Pogroms, expulsions and attempted genocide could have been avoided if Christians had not merely recited the creeds but understood them. Conversely, though, even the early rise of Christian hatred of the Jews was based on a historical fact: misunderstood, misinterpreted, indeed falsified in a despicable attempt to turn it against the Jews, but still a fact — Jesus had been killed. There never was a second of doubt, or even of hope, that he might have survived, did not need a resurrection and lived happily ever after. At 3.00 p.m. on 7 April AD 30, Jesus was dead.

If all of this Roman evidence, from Tacitus and his *Annals* to Constantine and the creeds, should fail to convince diehards among the sceptics, there remains a Jewish voice: Flavius Josephus. This man, briefly mentioned above, began his career as a Pharisee and priest (a rare combination, since most Pharisees never wanted to become priests), was made a general in the Jewish revolutionary forces that fought the Romans from AD 66 to 73, lost a battle in Galilee, was taken prisoner and prophesied to the commanding general of the Romans, Vespasian, that he would become Roman emperor, which he duly did in AD 69. Josephus was released and adopted into the imperial family of the Flavians (hence the name 'Flavius') and began to write books about Jewish history, trying to explain the Jews to the Romans and the Romans to his fellow Jews, who did not read his books, however, because to them Josephus had become a traitor. In his *Jewish Antiquities*, published in about AD 93, he mentions Jesus in a series of events that concerned Caiaphas and Pontius Pilate, and he has this to say about the crucifixion (*Antiquities* 18:63–64): 'And when Pilate sentenced him to the cross, following an accusation of our leading men, those who had loved him in the beginning did not cease to do so.'

This is straightforward enough. Josephus confirms that Jesus was crucified. He confirms that the Roman prefect Pontius Pilate was in charge, and therefore, by inference, that only he was responsible, and he mentions the leading members of the Sanhedrin as the accusers, or, to use the Roman legal term, the *delatores*. A Roman court procedure could not begin if there were no accuser or group of accusers. And then as now, those who press charges against someone for a supposed infringement of the law may not be held responsible for the final verdict – even if, as was the case with Jesus, the sentence passed by Pilate met the demands of the Sanhedrin. To put it another way, this sentence in the *Jewish Antiquities* is factually accurate and must count as a Jewish voice corroborating the Gospel evidence.

As it happens, Josephus had more to say about Jesus, and most scholars have assumed that this is too good to be true. A Jew who manifestly never became a Christian could not, or so these scholars assume, proclaim that 'he [Jesus] appeared to them [that is, to those who had loved him] alive again, on the third day, as the god-fearing prophets had pronounced it about him, together with countless miraculous deeds.' The Greek word for 'countless' is *myria*, as in the English 'myriad', and it can also mean 'ten thousand'. This is the text as we have it, with no trace of later alterations or additions in any of the surviving manuscripts, and Jewish-Christian studies have helped us to understand that this statement is not a later Christian insertion into the original text of Josephus but an utterly Jewish, very orthodox assessment of the situation. To begin with, Josephus records the result of his investigation – the followers of Jesus happily announced that the risen Jesus had appeared to them on the third day. And as we know, he also appeared to opponents and sceptics like his half-brother James and enemies like Sha'ul/Paul.

The second half of Josephus's statement is much more important, for it includes the miraculous deeds. They were never doubted in Jewish circles, as we noted above. The 'myriad' miracles is a rhetorical exaggeration but typical of Josephus's style. Then he mentions the prophets. Remember that Josephus was a Pharisaic priest. He knew his Bible better than most, and as someone who had spent three years as a young man with the Essenes, he also knew everything there was to know about messianic movements and prophecies. Therefore, his comment is a statement of fact. He knew that Isaiah had prophesied messianic miracles, he knew that they were mentioned in an Essene document and he knew the passage in Hosea 6:2: 'After two days he will revive us, on the third day he will raise us to live in his presence' (cf. Deuteronomy 32:39). Thus, he had no problem with such prophetic references – if that was what the followers of Jesus believed, he could see where they were coming from and could mention it without becoming a Christian himself.

One thing was clear to him, though, as a Jew and a Pharisee. These prophecies would have made no sense if the crucifixion had been a lie and if Jesus, half-beaten to death by the Romans even before he was crucified, had happily walked about as undead three days later. This is something no Jew could have taken seriously. The resurrection on the third day may have come as a surprise – it certainly did to Jesus' own disciples – since observant Jews expected the resurrection of all of the faithful dead much later, in the last days, rather than that of a single person ahead of all the others. But prophecies are not to be taken lightly, and those about the crucifixion (Isaiah 53:4–8, specific about a real, not an imagined, death in verse 8) and the resurrection of the faithful, from Isaiah 26:19 and Ezekiel 37:2–14 to Daniel 12:2 (taken up by Jesus in John 5:28–29), Hosea 6:2 and 2 Maccabees 7:9–14, were no laughing matter, either. No Jewish movement – and the first Christians were a Jewish movement – would have dared to proclaim the resurrection of a man professionally crucified by the Romans if he had not been truly dead. Josephus may not have known John's Gospel when he wrote his *Jewish Antiquities* – although he could have done – but in any case, John adds a further detail that he, the eyewitness, had observed (John 19:35–37). When a soldier thrust a lance into the side of Jesus, at once there was a flow of blood and water (19:34). This has been interpreted by medical experts as an indication of a person's death.

Josephus, who investigates his sources and accepts the death of Jesus, goes one step further and agrees that this Jesus, the doer of miraculous deeds whom Pontius Pilate had crucified and who had fulfilled ancient prophecies, was 'a wise man, if indeed one should call him a man', and he was the messiah. For this is what Josephus states, translated literally: 'The Messiah this one was.' Practically all the commentators have agreed that this is the crunch. Whatever else Josephus could have collected and thought about Jesus, no Jew could could have written this statement without being or becoming a Christian. But notice the past tense: 'This one *was* the Messiah'. No Christian forger or interpolator writes like this. '*Was*'? To Christians, he *is* the messiah, the Christ. In other words, the past tense indicates that this is what Josephus himself wrote, and not a later Christian falsifier of his text. And this helps us to see how a Jewish historian, who confirms the Christian testimony that Jesus had been truly crucified and truly appeared again alive on the third day, could have called him a past messiah. Josephus proclaims his own messiah, the Roman emperor Vespasian. When he realized that the prophecy in Genesis 49:10, about the ruler who will come from Judah, was used in vain by the Jewish revolutionaries in their war against the Romans, he switched sides. The new world domination would indeed come from the land of Judah, but the ruler, the messiah, would be a Roman rather than a Jew – the one who became emperor after his victories in the Jewish homeland (*Jewish Wars* 3:399). Tacitus and Suetonius, the two Roman historians who wrote about the period, agree (Tacitus, *Histories* 5:13,1–2; Suetonius, *Divus Vespasianus* 4:5). Vespasian was the ruler of the world who came from the land of Judah. In other words, Josephus was free to recall Isaiah 45:1–5, where another non-Jew, the Persian king Cyrus the Great – the saviour of true Judaism, the man who allowed the Jews to return from Babylonian captivity and even permitted the reconstruction of the First Temple – is hailed by God himself as the Messiah, the Christ. Josephus was a political animal if ever there was one. Calling Jesus the past messiah ('he *was*') and Vespasian the present one, he places his hopes in the future under Roman rule. And, as we know from the sources, even the rebuilding of the Second Temple, destroyed by Vespasian's son Titus in AD 70, was a distinct possibility in those days.

Finally, let us look at the question from a different

perspective. If Jesus was a messiah, but not the military warrior whom Josephus needed and proclaimed in Vespasian, what kind of messiah was he for him? Again, we know the answer. As we saw previously, many Jews expected at least two messiah figures, and the other one was not Davidic but Aaronic, from the line of the brother of Moses. He would be priestly rather than military. Some Jews thought that both would come in the last days, some thought that there would have to be a sequence, but in any case, Josephus, who had studied the teachings of the Pharisees, the Sadducees and the Essenes in his youth, was fully aware of these multifaceted expectations. The Essenes taught that the Aaronic Messiah would 'teach justice in the last days' (Damascus Document 6:11). He would win a decisive victory against the godless enemies, but without military means (Qumran fragment 1Q 28b 5, 20–26). Thus, Josephus, a man who knew these texts, a man who never became a Christian, or an Essene for that matter, rejected the Aaronic Messiah for his purposes, but accepted that he did exist in Jesus, 'who was the Messiah', and who, in accordance with ancient prophecies, performed miracles and even rose from the dead. As the Aaronic Messiah, Jesus was acceptable even to Josephus, but obviously he was not the messiah he wanted and needed. Even the well-attested testimony he had received from Christians did not turn him into a follower of the one messiah who, for him, was the wrong one, a past and spent force. Josephus demanded a military messiah. Everything else was past history. And if anyone should have suggested to him that Jesus was the Davidic, military messiah, he would have rejected him, since as such he had apparently failed. In other words, there was no Jewish messiah who mattered to him any more. It was a political decision, with religious overtones.

Today, we can understand that Jesus was both Aaronic and Davidic, through the ancestry of his mother Mary, and that he was confirmed in his Davidic ancestry through his adoption by Joseph, and we know that Jesus redefined the Davidic messiahship on the cross, when he prayed David's Psalm 22, the psalm that leads from forlornness and suffering to the final, messianic triumph:

> [1] My God, my God, why have you forsaken me?
> Why are you so far from helping me,
> from the words of my groaning?
> [2] O my God, I cry by day, but you do not answer;
> and by night, but find no rest.
>
> [3] Yet you are holy:
> enthroned on the praises of Israel.
> [4] In you our ancestors trusted:
> they trusted, and you delivered them.
> [5] To you they cried, and they were saved;
> in you they trusted, and were not put to shame.
>
> [6] But I am a worm, and not human:
> scorned by others, and despised by the people.
> [7] All who see me mock at me;
> they make mouths at me, they shake their heads;
>
> [8] 'Commit your cause to the LORD; let him deliver—
> let him rescue the one in whom he delights!'

[9] Yet it was you who took me from the womb;
you kept me safe on my mother's breast.

[10] On you I have been cast from birth,
and since my mother bore me you have been my God.
[11] Do not be far from me,
for trouble is near and there is no one to help.

[12] Many bulls encircle me,
strong bulls of Bashan surround me;
[13] They open their mouths wide at me,
like a ravening and roaring lion.

[14] I am poured out like water,
and all my bones are out of joint;
my heart is like wax; it is melted within my breast;
[15] my mouth is dried up like a potsherd,
and my tongue sticks to my jaws;
you lay me in the dust of death.

[16] For dogs are all around me;
a company of evildoers encircles me.
They have pierced my hands and my feet.
[17] I can count all my bones.
They stare and gloat over me;
[18] they divide my clothes among themselves;
and for my clothing they cast lots.

[19] But you, O Lord, do not be far away!
O my help, come quickly to my aid!
[20] Deliver my soul from the sword,
my life from the power of the dog!
[21] Save me from the mouth of the lion!

From the horns of the wild oxen you have rescued me.
²² I will tell of your name to my brothers and sisters;
In the midst of the congregation I will praise you:

²³You who fear the Lord, praise him!
All you offspring of Jacob, glorify him;
stand in awe of him, all you offspring of Israel!
²⁴ For he did not despise or abhor
the affliction of the afflicted;
he did not hide his face from me,
but heard when I cried to him.

²⁵ From you comes my praise in the great congregation;
my vows I will pay before those who fear him.
²⁶ The poor shall eat and be satisfied;
those who seek him shall praise the Lord.
May your hearts live forever!

²⁷ All the ends of the earth shall remember
and turn to the Lord;
and all the families of the nations
shall worship before him.
²⁸ For dominion belongs to the Lord,
and he rules over the nations.

²⁹ To him, indeed, shall all who sleep in the earth bow down;
before him shall bow all who go down to the dust,
and I shall live for him.
³⁰ Posterity will serve him;
future generations will be told about the Lord,
³¹ and proclaim his deliverance to a people yet unborn,
saying that he has done it.

Josephus drew his own conclusions. His hopes were not eschatological, but rooted in the here and now, in his own survival, in the acceptance of Roman supremacy and in his efforts to salvage a Jewish future under the Roman, 'messianic', emperors. So again, we may regret that Josephus, who had come so close, rejected Jesus for political, even religious, reasons that are, from a Christian viewpoint, understandable if not acceptable. But in the end, there is no way around it. His statement about Jesus is true to character; it is pure Josephus, and we should continue to read it as an authentic testimony to the crucifixion and to the resurrection – the earliest such testimony outside the New Testament.

As for the crucifixion and the death on the cross, the number of eyewitnesses available to an investigative Josephus was quite remarkable, and they included Jesus' opponents, who would have made sure that he was dead when they left the site of the crucifixion. If we look at just Mark's Gospel, there were the high priest and the scribes (Mark 15:31) and the people passing by who mocked and ridiculed Jesus (15:29), probably the same people who pretended they misunderstood his dying words (15:35). But there was also Simon of Cyrene, who had carried the horizontal beam of the cross to Golgotha (15:21); there were Mary his mother, Mary Magdalene, Mary the mother of James and Joses, together with Salome (15:40) and other women, and the beloved disciple (John 19:25–27). Watching from a distance, probably from the nearby city wall, there were the disciples and others (Luke 23:49) – different people, watching and listening from different positions. Perhaps the most striking witnesses to his death on the cross are two members of the Sanhedrin, Joseph of Arimathea and Nicodemus. Joseph, a man of repute and a 'secret' disciple, asked Pilate for the body to bury it in his own family tomb, and Pilate, not surprisingly, granted him permission. All four Gospels agree in their reports, and John adds that Joseph was joined by Nicodemus (John 19:38–42). Nicodemus, a Pharisee who had followed Jesus' career closely, arrived with a mixture of myrrh and aloe, valuable enough for a royal burial. It is of course inconceivable that neither of them should have noticed, during the elaborate burial preparations, that Jesus was not dead and needed medical treatment instead of a procedure that covered the head and mouth and would have smothered him if he had not been dead already. Briefly, those who deny that Jesus died on the cross live in a world of their own myth-making.

7

DID JESUS REALLY RISE
FROM THE DEAD?

The vast majority of Jews were expecting a resurrection, and as we saw in the previous chapter, the thinker and historian Flavius Josephus was no exception. Only one Jewish movement, the Sadducees, remained on the sidelines as they refused to believe anything they could not find in the Torah, the five books of Moses. Josephus and the New Testament concur in their accounts. The Sadducees, the priestly caste of the Temple, did not believe in the resurrection. It was of course a problem entirely of their own making, as God's capability to raise the dead is unmistakably referred to in the last book of the Torah, Deuteronomy 32:39. Everyone else could trace the line that went from Deuteronomy to Isaiah 26:19, Ezekiel 37:7–14, Daniel 12:2 and Hosea 6:2, looking forward to a triumphant resurrection in the last days.

The Essenes set down their hopes in one of their writings, which has survived as fragments in their caves at

Qumran – it is a scroll we have encountered before, 4Q 521. Here it is quoted with square brackets around damaged words that have had to be reconstructed:

'[For the heav]ens and the earth will listen to His Messiah, [and all w]hich is in them will not turn away from the commandments of the holy ones. Strengthen yourselves, you who seek the Lord, in His service. All you who are hopeful in your hearts, will you not find the Lord in this? For the Lord will seek the pious and call the righteous by name. Over the humble His spirit will hover and will renew the faithful in His strength. And He will honour the pious on the throne of His eternal kingdom. He will set prisoners free, opening the eyes of the blind, raising up those who are bo[wed down]. And f[or]ever shall [I] hold fast [to the h]opeful and pious... And the fr[uit] will not be delayed. And the Lord shall do glorious things which have never been achieved, [just as He promised]. For He shall heal the pierced, He shall revive the dead, and bring good news to the poor.'

The final fragment underlines the bodily resurrection: 'And He will open the tombs.' Another Qumran scroll, the 'Thanksgiving Hymns', confirms the continuous presence of the age-old prophetic spirit among the contemporaries of Jesus: 'You [the Lord] have purified man from sin, so that he may be holy for you, with no abominable uncleanness and no guilty wickedness, so that he may be one with the children of your truth and share in the lot of your holy ones, so that bodies gnawed by worms may be raised from the dust, to the counsel of your truth' (1QH 19[11]:10–14).

Later, in the Talmud, the erroneous teaching of the Sadducees is rebuked from a pharisaic perspective: 'And you shall know that I am the Lord, when I open your tombs, and bring you up from your graves, O my people' ('Taanit' 2a/2b). The Talmud thus interprets Ezekiel 37:13, which it quotes and expands, as the prophecy of a bodily resurrection. Another talmudic text, 'Ketubboth' 111b, likens the rising bodies to grain, which is buried naked but will rise clad in splendour. The writings of the Talmud contain some teachings that go back to the time of Jesus and before, but they were published in the sixth century, long after the resurrection of Jesus. This is remarkable, for the talmudic collectors could easily have excluded or deleted all references to the physical resurrection if the resurrection of Jesus had bothered them. The spontaneous reaction of some of the high priest's people who claimed that the disciples had stolen the body of Jesus (Matthew 27:62–66; 28:11–15), incredibly desperate as it was, did not lead to a revision of the ancient conviction that there will be a resurrection, and that it will not be spiritual but physical. And as we saw in the previous chapter, someone like Flavius Josephus could easily believe that Jesus had indeed died and had indeed risen, bodily, from the dead, and yet still not become a Christian. Modern Jewish thinkers like Pinchas Lapide have followed Josephus in this respect. They accept that Jesus truly rose from the dead, as a righteous Jew who simply preceded the pious of his people. But they do not see how this will make him the one and only Messiah, the one and only saviour, and God incarnate who came to suffer for the sins of humankind. The historicity of the resurrection and faith in Jesus Christ do not appear to form a natural sequence in everyone's eyes. It obviously takes more to become convinced, and Christians should see this as a positive challenge: their faith in Jesus would be somewhat deficient if it depended on the results of the historical sciences. It is, after all, a faith and not a mathematical equation.

And yet the historical trustworthiness of the resurrection accounts does matter, as they are part and parcel of the New Testament's message: not legends but real, witnessed, researched events are the basis of the Christian proclamation. A Pharisee, the Jew Sha'ul/Paul, who insisted that he remained a Pharisee even as a follower of Christ (Acts 22:6; cf. Philippians 3:5), pointed this out:

> 'Now if Christ is proclaimed as raised from the dead, how can some of you say there is no resurrection of the dead? If there is no resurrection of the dead, then Christ has not been raised; and if Christ has not been raised, then our proclamation has been in vain and your faith has been in vain. We are even found to be misrepresenting God, because we testified of God that he raised Christ – whom he did not raise if it is true that the dead are not raised. For if the dead are not raised, then Christ has not been raised. If Christ has not been raised, your faith is futile, and you are still in your sins. Then those who have also died in Christ have perished. If for this life only we have hoped in Christ, we are of all people most to be pitied. But in fact Christ has been raised from the dead, the first fruits of those who have died'
> (1 Corinthians 15:12–20).

For someone like Paul, highly intelligent, well trained academically in Tarsus and by Gamaliel the Great in Jerusalem, the resurrection of Jesus the Messiah was of course a bodily resurrection, not a visionary experience or hallucination. Since all the Jewish documents, from the prophets to the Qumran scrolls, talk of a resurrection exclusively in terms of risen bodies and open tombs, he does not once in his letters mention the empty tomb of Christ. To him it was self-evident, as it was to his readers, that the tomb was empty on Easter morning, so he refrains from stating the obvious. It was a precondition rather than a piece of evidence: no resurrection without an empty tomb.

All these Jews knew something else. A risen body is a new body, and while this body is a physical reality, able to speak, walk, eat and drink, it is also a new creation. No one had been raised to this new life before – when Jesus brought back to life Lazarus, the young man from Nain and the daughter of Jairus, these were reawakenings of people who would have to die a normal human death eventually. His followers simply had to come to terms with the unknown reality of a risen messiah. Only one thing was certain to them, as readers of Ezekiel 37:7–14. They would not be able to recognize the risen Christ from his physical appearance, since the old bones will be covered by new sinews, new flesh and new skin. They took this for granted – we may be surprised that they did not recognize him but they themselves were not. Mary Magdalene takes him for a gardener, and only when he pronounces her name in a way she recognizes does she turn round and address him as 'Rabbuni', Master (John 20:14–18). When the two disciples, Cleopas and his nameless companion, meet the risen Christ on their way home to Emmaus, they do not recognize him until he is at home with them, taking the bread and blessing and breaking it in a characteristic manner (Luke 24:30–31). 'Doubting' Thomas, who was not present when Jesus revealed himself to the other disciples, wants to see the marks of the nails in his wrists. ('Hands' is a mistranslation – the Greek word *cheir* can mean both hand and arm, but as we know that a crucified person was not nailed through the palms, which would have been torn apart immediately under the weight of the body, 'wrists', or broadly 'arms', would be the better translation). And he wants to see the wound in his side (John 20:24–25). Why? After all, the others had seen these marks of the crucifixion already. Thomas, however, applies the art of lateral thinking: a risen body is pure, the new flesh will not show any traces of the person's life, no wounds, no warts, no scars. In those days, Jews practised the second burial – after several months, when the flesh had decayed, the tomb was reopened and the bones were placed in a bone-casket, an 'ossuary', awaiting the bodily resurrection according to Ezekiel 37:7–14, when new, pure flesh and skin would be put on them. These ossuaries were often inscribed with the name of the reburied person. The ossuary of a contemporary of Jesus, Yehonan Ben Hazkul, included the heelbone with the nail of his crucifixion still inside – the nail had fishhooked and could not be pulled out, so Yehonan was reburied in his ossuary with the crucifier's nail still in his heelbone: the only archaeological evidence to date, among numerous literary references, of a Roman crucifixion. So even a crucified man was not excluded from the preparations for the resurrection in the last days. But Jesus had risen before his bones could be placed in an ossuary. What would his new body look like? Were the others merely imagining that the old wounds were still there? On a newly created, resurrected body, they should not be visible, after all.

Thomas wanted to see for himself. The risen Christ entered the room although the doors were shut. Miraculous, perhaps, but then again, even the most observant of Jews did not know what a resurrected body was able to do. Enlightened as they were, they accepted what they saw. The next step was decisive: Jesus parted his cloak and Thomas saw the wounds. He knew that they should not have been there, on the pure skin of a risen person's body, but they were. And so he understood that Jesus, the Risen One, still remained the Crucified One. His resurrection does not negate or nullify his crucifixion. The risen Christ remains the crucified Jesus. Thomas does not even have to touch the wound – John in his Gospel does not say he does. It is merely the interpretative addition of many famous works of art that has made us think otherwise. Overwhelmed by this sudden insight, he said what no Jew had ever before said about another Jew: 'My Lord and my God.' Some critics have opined that this is the evangelist's theological invention. But having looked at the context of the crucifixion from a Jewish perspective, we know better. The words uttered by Thomas turn out to be very devout, a very Jewish statement. At this one moment, old prophecies and experienced truth fall into place and become one.

It is impossible to escape the sober insistence, free of all those legendary additions one so often finds in Egyptian and Greek myths, on the observed reality of these events. Take Peter, for example, a fisherman from Capernaum, who clung on to his human hopes so firmly, not wishing Jesus to die, that he raised a sword in the Garden of Gethsemane to defend him. He was courageous enough to follow him into the high priest's courtyard and humanly frail enough to deny him three times. But he learned his lesson, and much later, when he met the Roman centurion Cornelius in Caesarea Maritima, he convinced this experienced professional soldier by his eyewitness testimony, which includes an unmistakable reference to the physical body of the risen Christ: 'We are witnesses to all that he did both in Judea and in Jerusalem. They put him to death by hanging him on a tree; but God raised him on the third day and allowed him to appear, not to all the people but to us who were chosen by God as witnesses, and who ate and drank with him after he rose from the dead' (Acts 10:39–41). Luke, the author of the book of Acts, knew what he was doing when he included this snippet of information about food. In his Gospel, he had made the same point when he reported that the risen Christ was given a piece of broiled fish 'and took it and ate in their presence' (Luke 24:42–43). Both Luke's Gospel and Acts are dedicated to Theophilus, called 'His Excellency' (in Greek, *krátistos*), a professional term that describes a high-ranking Roman civil servant. Theophilus and the commanding officer Cornelius shared the same classical upbringing of educated Greeks and Romans. For them, there was no life after death, nor a resurrection of the body. All they could envisage was a separation of body and soul and the possibility that the soul might hover on a kind of 'island of the blessed'. The testimony of the eyewitnesses convinced them. Jesus was different; his resurrection was real, not just spiritual. He could eat and drink. Cornelius was baptized and his whole household with him. Theophilus, who had read the Gospel, which was written for him so that he might 'know the truth concerning the things about which you have been instructed' (Luke 1:4), obviously understood and accepted the eyewitness accounts, for he agreed to allow the sequel to the Gospel, the book of Acts, to be dedicated to him as well (Acts 1:1). He would have refused to accept volume number two, and Luke would not have written it for him, if he had had any doubts. Two educated Romans in leading positions are convinced by what they heard and read, despite everything they had learned during their Greco-Roman upbringing. No mean achievement, given the circumstances. And it is these circumstances to which we now have to turn.

Jewish society was male-orientated. Jesus was verging on the revolutionary when he allowed women into his closest company. Mary Magdalene, perhaps the most famous, was only one of them; Mary and Martha of Bethany also played significant roles, and with the exception of the beloved disciple, the remaining followers in the immediate vicinity of the cross were all women. Two days later, on the third day, the first visitors to the empty tomb were again exclusively women. All four Gospels agree on this point. At the empty tomb, the different Gospels name different women, focusing on those known to them and to their first readers, but even in John's Gospel, where only Mary Magdalene is mentioned by name, we learn that there were several women at the empty tomb: 'We do not know where they have laid him,' she says to Peter, speaking for a group that is still not capable of grasping the unexpected resurrection of Jesus. To the historian, this agreement among the sources offers a beacon of insight. For in male-orientated Jewish society, the witness of women did not count. What they said would not be acceptable in court; it had no legal value. To put it bluntly, they might as well not say anything. But God allows women to be the first bearers of the news that the tomb was empty; only then can the men act and check for themselves. Again, it is not a man but two women, Mary Magdalene and 'the other Mary', who are granted the first encounter with the risen Christ on Easter Day (Matthew 28:8–10; cf. John 20:14–18), before Peter and before the two Emmaus disciples. In social and legal terms, this was an embarrassment; in historical terms, though, it underlines the fact that these accounts were not invented.

The issue of the female witnesses was a problem for Paul, which he later had to solve. It occurs in his first letter to the Corinthians, where he gives his readers a list of resurrection witnesses (1 Corinthians 15: 5–9). The Corinthians were in need of a document that they could use to convince themselves and those they wanted to convert that Jesus had truly risen and had been seen by trustworthy witnesses. Thus, there is not a single woman in Paul's list. He begins with Peter, then mentions the remaining apostles as a group, then more than five hundred at one time, 'most of whom are still alive', who could therefore be visited and interviewed. (Some modern translations unfortunately falsify the text by writing that

Jesus appeared to 'more than five hundred brothers and sisters', but there are no sisters in the Greek text. Paul really does concentrate on male witnesses alone.) Then Paul mentions James, which is a strategically intelligent move since people knew that James had been a sceptic, if not an opponent, before he met the risen Christ. Finally, he lists another opponent, one who had actively persecuted the Christians: Paul himself. It is a list that was devised with a clear purpose: to strengthen the committed and convince the sceptics. Go and interview them, Paul implies, and do not trust those rumours that Jesus only appeared to his devoted followers. James and I, Paul, are proof that that is not the case.

Paul was no misogynist, no hater or despiser of women, as some have read into this and other passages. He worked with them (for example, Prisca/Priscilla, who is mentioned before her husband Aquila, as a fellow worker in Romans 16:3, and also in 1 Corinthians 16:19 as the leader of a house church with her husband); he trusted them as community leaders (Lydia and Nympha as the leaders of two house churches – Acts 16:40; Colossians 4:15); he calls one the deacon of the church at Cenchrea (Phoebe in Romans 16:1) and mentions another as 'prominent among the apostles' (Junias in Romans 16:7). It is an impressive list in its own right, and those who think that Paul did not like women should think again and come to terms with the fact that his occasional criticism of women in the church may have had different origins, after all. As for the resurrection appearances in 1 Corinthians 15, we have seen why he did not mention them – for perfectly reasonable, strategic reasons. But the Gospel authors did not tailor their writings in the same way: they set out to write historical accounts. And thus, they conscientiously mentioned the women as being the first witnesses to the empty tomb and, above all, to the resurrection. To the professional historian, then, this is the strongest indication that this is the way it really was. The four Gospel authors, all men themselves, would have been more than happy to avoid all reference to the women whose testimony was almost counterproductive. But as historians, they wrote down the facts as they really happened, even mentioning names.

It seems the early church understood the problem. When men like Marcion tried to advocate the use of only one Gospel in the mid-second century – Luke's Gospel in Marcion's case, but 'purified' of all pro-Jewish passages because he was an anti-Semite – the others agreed to differ and insisted on a four-Gospel canon. By doing so, they were following an old rule of Jewish and Greco-Roman practice regarding witnesses. Deuteronomy 17:6 and 19:15 provide the first biblical references: 'A charge must be established on the evidence of two or three witnesses' (19:15). Jesus expands on this: 'But if he will not listen, take one or two others with you, so that every case may be settled on the evidence of two or three witnesses' (Matthew 18:16). And Paul concurs: 'As the scripture says, "Every charge must be established on the evidence of two or three witnesses"' (2 Corinthians 13:1). This legal requirement was fulfilled when the church collected three Gospels written from a comparable perspective, the so-called 'synoptics', Matthew, Mark and Luke, and added John's personal account for good measure. Thus, there were not only two or three, but four male witnesses, who confirmed in writing that the women had been telling the truth. The legal obligation had been met, and we can show from surviving papyrological evidence that the Gospels were distributed in collections of at least two, and very soon of all four, from the mid-second century at the latest.

The women, along with all the disciples, disappointed and utterly without hope from the afternoon of Good Friday to the night of Holy Saturday, the darkest day of their lives, were in no position to create hope out of nothing, against all expectations and against their own Jewish belief that nothing could possibly happen before the end of time. To their amazement and initial disbelief, it did. When they realized what had happened, how did they respond? It is remarkable that they did not overreact but enjoyed forty days of reflection, and of communion with the risen Christ, before they began their mission among their fellow Jews, as Jesus had told them to do immediately before he left them (Acts 1:3–11; cf. Matthew 28:18–20). The original ending of Mark's Gospel makes this point brilliantly. When Mark wrote, he knew of course that the women at the empty tomb had told the others about their experience. But at first, silence was the appropriate reaction: 'They said nothing to anyone, for they were afraid' (Mark 16:8). The second half of Mark's last sentence should be translated differently: '...for they were seized by holy fear'. They had understood that God had shown his presence in the real, historical world, that he had performed his greatest deed, the raising of his incarnate son. Throughout Mark's Gospel, and frequently in the Old Testament, people are gripped by holy fear when they recognize God's presence among them. Peter, James and John, for example, saw Moses and Elijah appear to Jesus and heard God's voice on the Mount of the Transfiguration, and Peter 'did not know what to say – they were so terrified' (Mark 9:6). But the miracle of the resurrection was in a different category, and thus Mark concludes his Gospel on a note of silence.

The women may have spoken to Peter and the others half an hour or even a couple of hours later: that was not his point. Even a historical account may be allowed to end with a dramatic dash or ellipsis, and this is what Mark's Greek sentence achieves: his last word is *gar*, 'for...', and no Greek writer had dared to conclude a text like that before (although he was copied a couple of times by later authors). It means, of course, that Mark knew that the story of the risen Christ was to go on and that he could leave the details to others writing after him. As early as about AD 120, Christians failed to grasp his message and wrote additional endings, which have been preserved, between brackets, in our Gospel editions. Yet the greatness of Mark as an author of Greek, Hellenistic historiography was combined with his humility in faith. For him, the resurrection of Jesus Christ was much more than an event in human history, well documented and testified to by eyewitnesses. It was also a reaffirmation of faith, faith in the old prophecy that Jesus truly was and is 'God with us' (cf. Matthew 1:23). We would do well to keep this side of the reality of his resurrection in mind.

8

WHO DID JESUS THINK HE WAS?

Wasn't he just a good man and a charismatic leader?

Jesus talked about himself in numerous Gospel passages, and often enough, his opponents confronted him about who he was. Among these incidents, one stands out, as it combines a lack of understanding on the part of his disappointed followers with his attempt to explain things to them. It is the story of the two Emmaus disciples, briefly referred to in the previous chapter. On the afternoon of Easter Day, the two of them have left Jerusalem and are on their way home to a village called Emmaus, some 8.6 kilometres westwards − which has been identified, thanks to ongoing excavations, as a site near the ruins of Qaloniyeh, below the terraces of Mozah (Joshua 18:26). Someone they do not recognize joins them. Luke, the author of this account (Luke 24:13−35), tells his readers that the man is the risen Jesus, but the two travellers are not aware of this. As we saw in the previous chapter, Jesus' newly resurrected body could not be recognized as such. 'What are you discussing with each other while you walk along?' he asks them. One of them, Cleopas, replies: 'Are you only a stranger in Jerusalem who does not know these things that have taken place there in these days?' Jesus pretends to be ignorant: 'What things?' And the explanation given by Cleopas, who assumes that their new companion really is ignorant of recent events, sums up what people of good will thought about Jesus: 'The things about Jesus of Nazareth, who was a prophet mighty in deed and word before God and all the people, and how our chief priests and leaders handed him over to be condemned to death and crucified him.' (Our translations are slightly misleading without commentary: the Emmaus disciples, like everyone else, knew of course that the high priest and his people did not crucify Jesus as they had no legal right to do so. Only the Romans carried out crucifixions, and Luke himself makes this unmistakably clear in his account of the hearings before Pontius Pilate, the sentencing and the crucifixion itself.) Cleopas goes on: 'But we had hoped that he was the one to redeem Israel. And besides all this, it is now the third day since these things took place. Moreover, some women of our group astounded us. They were at the tomb early this morning, and when they did not find his body there, they came back and told us that they had indeed seen an apparition [not a vision as most translations have it] of angels who said that he was alive. Some of those who were with us went to the tomb and found it just as the women had said; but they did not see him.'

These two disciples, not among the twelve, but members of the wider circle of followers who had left Jerusalem before the news of Jesus' first appearances could reach them, sum up who Jesus was for them: in the first place, he was a prophet, mighty in deed and word. This was a starting point, and it recalls the disciples' summing up of public opinion as they travelled with Jesus from Bethsaida to Caesarea Philippi. 'Who do people say the Son of Man is?' Jesus had asked. 'Some say John the Baptist, but others Elijah, and still others Jeremiah, or one of the prophets' (Matthew 16:14). The Emmaus disciples add 'mighty in deed and word'. The deeds, those messianic miracles, already single him out among the prophets, and the words, like the Sermon on the Mount, his parables and his eschatological teaching, confirm his unique position among them. Cleopas, along with his companion and all the others for whom he spoke, had drawn his conclusion: 'We had hoped that he was the one to redeem Israel.' Here we have it once again – the messianic expectancy so common among Jews at the time: redemption and deliverance, as it should have come with the Davidic Messiah, vanquishing enemies (the Roman occupying forces) from outside and from within, and establishing his messianic rule over and against the corrupt, pro-Roman elite of the high priest and his entourage at the Temple.

Peter had tried to initiate the final messianic battle in the Garden of Gethsemane when he took his sword and cut off the right ear of Malchus, the high priest's servant. According to Jewish law, a priest, and the high priest in particular, had to be physically perfect, without any visible blemishes. Any such defect would end his career. The servant, of noble descent himself (Malchus means 'the royal one'), represented the high priest. When Peter cut off a part of his face, he did not do so by mistake. He simply tried to force Jesus' hand: if the high priest was rendered unfit for office, his rule was ended and the messianic battle could begin. Jesus had to explain, not for the first time, that he was not the military messiah that the majority of Jews expected, including Peter; and he restored the ear. Yes, indeed: Jesus had come to redeem Israel – but not by brute force, in a gory battle, as even the ultra-pious Essenes had expected. How to make sense of it all? The disciples went into hiding after the crucifixion, and, understandably, the two Emmaus disciples were disappointed and dejected too. Their messiah and redeemer had been crucified by their arch-enemies, the Romans.

Cleopas knew of the first accounts of the empty tomb, but could he trust the stories about Jesus appearing alive? After all, before he and his companion left Jerusalem, only women had talked of it, and we know how little a woman's witness counted among Jews – even among the wider circle of Jesus' followers, it seems. To summarize at this point: Jesus was seen as a prophet. More than a prophet, he was a man of messianic miracles and was regarded as the messianic redeemer by his followers until his death on the cross. After that came disappointment. Even Peter himself may well have wondered if his courageous words at Caesarea Philippi, when he had pronounced Jesus the messiah and the Son of God, had been a mistake. Then, still a few miles from Emmaus, Jesus takes over. '"Oh, how foolish you are, and how slow of heart to believe all that the prophets have declared! Was it not necessary that the Messiah should suffer these things and then enter into his glory?" Then, beginning with Moses and all the prophets, he interpreted to them the things about himself in all the scriptures' (Luke 24:25–27). Many readers of Luke's Gospel would have been immensely grateful if he had done them the favour of adding several pages to his scroll, detailing these 'things in all the scriptures'. We have already seen, in the preceding chapters, what Jesus meant. His image of himself was not of his own making. He strictly followed the line that had begun when God's messenger, the angel Gabriel, had told his mother that he would be called 'the Son of the Most High', 'the Son of God' (Luke 1:32–35). Jesus insists that Cleopas and his companion should have understood this, and everything else that followed, all along. After all, he had explained it often enough. Much earlier, at Caesarea Philippi in northern Galilee, he had told his disciples that he was truly the Messiah/Christ and Son of the Most High, confirming Peter's proclamation and telling Peter that he owed this insight to 'my Father in heaven' (Matthew 16:17), but adding, soon after, that 'he must go to Jerusalem and undergo great suffering at the hands of the elders and chief priests and scribes, and be killed, and on the third day be raised'.

Many New Testament critics have interpreted this as Matthew's invention – after all, how could Jesus prophesy future events? But we have seen that he could, and that the critics, ideologically biased against Jesus as a prophet, are merely cut off from Jewish thought.

Whether or not the majority of contemporary Jews understood this before Easter — and most of them obviously did not — the ancient prophetic voice predicted the suffering Messiah. Isaiah, the greatest of the prophets, had described it in gruesome detail in chapter 53 of his book. Mel Gibson's controversial *The Passion of the Christ* alienated many viewers with its excruciatingly detailed depiction of the tortures that preceded the crucifixion. But seconds before the actual film begins, there is a passage from Isaiah, in white letters on the black screen: 'He was wounded for our transgressions, crushed for our iniquities, upon him was the punishment that made us whole, and by his bruises we are healed' (Isaiah 53:5). If this was not just to be meaningless poetry it had to be fulfilled in the passion of Jesus. He himself certainly lived with this prophecy and it was one of the prophecies he explained to the Emmaus disciples.

Obviously, the two on their way home to Emmaus were disappointed in their messianic hopes, and it follows that the passages about the suffering Messiah would have played a central role in Jesus' explanation of scripture. But the image of himself that he gave them was chronological. It began with Moses, and this was the yardstick, as we saw: Moses and the Torah were paramount. What these five books had to say was even more binding than Isaiah. Thus, Jesus knew and explained that there was nothing in the Torah that proved Isaiah wrong, but that, on the contrary, the nucleus of the prophet's words could be deduced from these five books. In John's Gospel, he challenges his opponents in Jerusalem with a reference to scriptures in general and Moses in particular:

'You search the scriptures because you think that in them you have eternal life; and it is they that testify on my behalf. Yet you refuse to come to me to have life. I do not accept glory from human beings. But I know that you do not have the love of God in you. I have come in my Father's name, and you do not accept me; if another comes in his own name, you will accept him. How can you believe when you accept glory from one another and do not seek the glory that comes from the one who alone is God? Do not think that I will accuse you before the Father; your accuser is Moses, on whom you have set your hope. If you believed Moses, you would believe me, for he wrote about me. But if you do not believe what he wrote, how will you believe what I say?' (John 5:39–47).

Clearly, the Gospels do not disregard the controversies. Often enough, Jesus faced an audience that was hostile not as a matter of principle, but because they could not – yet – see how someone like Jesus, a Galilean building worker's adoptive son, could be the triumphant, military messiah they were all expecting. In Jerusalem, the city of the Temple, they even hesitated to accept the verdict of the northern Jews, that he was at least one of the prophets, or, in other words, a messianic precursor. Therefore, Jesus had to explain and defend his position, and in the manner of the time, he does so with uncompromising words in a language that sometimes sounds aggressive to our sensitive postmodern ears.

The strategic necessity of going back to Moses and his writings, to the Torah, was understood and emulated by Paul. He spells it out in his letter to the Romans

(5:12–13): 'Therefore, just as sin came into the world through one man [Adam, Genesis 3:19], and death came through sin [Genesis 2:17], so death spread to all because all have sinned.' Death exercised dominion from Adam to Moses, even over those whose sins were not likened to the transgression of Adam, who is a type of the one who was to come. Adam is understood as the sinning prefiguration of the sinless Christ, the first man created by God, who failed where Jesus, the Son of God and God incarnate, triumphed: 'For since death came through a human being, the resurrection of the dead has also come through a human being. For as all die in Adam, so all will be made alive in Christ,' as Paul explains elsewhere (1 Corinthians 15:21–22). This kind of reasoning, which may look unfamiliar today, was well known to rabbis and their audiences. Paul's technique of describing a 'typology', like the one of Adam and Jesus, even has a traditional Hebrew name. It was called *qal va-chomer*, or 'from the simple to the difficult', and was the first of the seven rules of interpretation described by Hillel, the great rabbinical teacher whose school of thought gave rise to Gamaliel and his pupil Paul. We tend to pass over these passages, as they look complicated and distant. It was, however, an integral part of Jewish life and thought to think and write in such terms in those days (and it still is today among the rabbis), and we will understand more about Jesus' self-image, opposition towards him and support for him, such as that from Paul, if we take Jesus, Paul and the others seriously as Jews. There are numerous similar examples. Returning to Emmaus, one important point remains: the glory of which Jesus speaks to Cleopas and his companion. What exactly does this mean? Where and how did Jesus see himself as glorious? Most of us have seen medieval paintings that depict Jesus in his apparel of royal glory. But could the two Emmaus disciples make sense of this 'glory'? Was it a human or a God-given side of Jesus' identity?

Throughout the Old Testament, 'glory' is one of God's qualities, sometimes even one of his emanations, as in Exodus 24:16–17: 'The glory of the Lord settled on Mount Sinai, and the cloud covered it for six days; on the seventh day he called to Moses out of the cloud. Now the appearance of the glory of the Lord was like a devouring fire on the top of the mountain in the sight of the people of Israel.' Or take Exodus 40:34: 'Then the cloud covered the tent of meeting, and the glory of the Lord filled the tabernacle.' The glory of God does not always arrive in a cloud. The prophet Ezekiel, for example, describes an experience that comes quite close to a vision of the Trinity: God the Father, Son and Holy Spirit: 'Then the hand of the Lord was upon me; and he said to me: "Rise up, go out into the valley, and there I will speak with you." So I rose up and went out into the valley; and the glory of the Lord stood there, like the glory that I had seen by the river Chebar; and I fell on my face. The Spirit entered into me, and set me on my feet; and he spoke with me...' (Ezekiel 3:22–24). Jews who heard Jesus talk about divine glory knew therefore that he was referring to such passages from the Torah and the Prophets. 'Those who are ashamed of me and of my words in this adulterous and sinful generation,' he says in Mark 8:38, 'of them the Son of Man will also be ashamed when he comes in the glory of his Father, with the holy angels.' Using one of his favourite titles for himself, 'Son of Man', he appeals to another prophetic voice, that of Daniel, where the familiar clouds from the Torah also play a role: 'As I watched in the night visions, I saw one like a Son of Man, coming with the clouds of heaven. And he came to the Ancient of Days and was presented before him. To him was given dominion and glory and kingship, that all peoples, nations and languages should serve him. His dominion is an everlasting dominion that shall not pass away, and his kingship is one that shall never be destroyed' (Daniel 7:13–14).

By using the title 'Son of Man', not only here but many times in the Gospels, Jesus explains that he is the Messiah, God's Anointed, who has come in God's glory – indeed, that he too possesses God's glory. And Jesus obviously plays on the double meaning of the Hebrew and Aramaic words. For 'a son of man' can mean 'a human being', a human child. Through Mary, this of course also applied to Jesus. And in the Old Testament, Psalm 8:4 uses the expression: 'What is a human being, that you are mindful of him, and the Son of Man, that you care for him?' The prophet Ezekiel, certainly not the Messiah, is also called 'son of man' by God (Ezekiel 2:1; 3:1, etc.). In Jesus both meanings merge into one for the first time. He is both Mary's son and the Son of God in his glory, and Jesus wants his audience to understand that this is how he sees himself.

It is perhaps in John's Gospel where he is challenged most vehemently by those who see things differently, some time before the crucifixion (John 10:22–39, etc.). Some ask him: 'How long will you keep us in suspense? If you are the Messiah, tell us plainly.' Jesus answers: 'I have told you, and you do not believe. The works that I do in my Father's name testify to me, but you do not believe, because you do not belong to my sheep. My sheep hear my voice. I know them, and they follow me. I give them eternal life, and they will never perish… I and the Father are one.' This, to them, is blasphemy. Far from accepting his claim, they take up stones to stone him: 'It is not for a good work that we are going to stone you, but for blasphemy, because you, though only a human being, are making yourself God.' Jesus insists that his deeds, all of them messianic, as we saw in a previous chapter, prove that 'the Father is in me and I am in the Father'. Basically, he argues as he argued when he showed the disciples of John the Bapist that he truly is the one 'who was to come'. John the Baptist and his followers, however, were willing to trust him — at the very least, they were open-minded. For the opponents in Jerusalem and elsewhere, on the other hand, the messianic miracles and deeds were not the solution but the problem. If Jesus was the Davidic Messiah they expected, the deliverer who would assemble the angelic hosts, why then did he not do any of the things they were expecting? Why was he walking about with a group of harmless-looking disciples and yet making a claim about his godship that sounded unambiguous enough? To them, it was blasphemy. Some time later, the high priest Caiaphas, who never for a moment doubted that all the miracles had been performed, again accused Jesus of blasphemy: 'Are you the Messiah, the Son of the Blessed One?' Caiaphas asked, and Jesus answered: 'I am, and you will see the Son of Man seated at the right hand of the

Power, and coming with the clouds of heaven' — two unmistakable allusions to the glory of God himself. 'Then the High Priest tore his clothes and said: "Why do we still need witnesses? You have heard his blasphemy! What is your decision?" All of them condemned him as deserving death' (Mark 14:61–64).

On the road to Emmaus, Jesus explained these things to Cleopas and the other disciple and they listened patiently. Luke makes it plain enough that there was no flash of sudden insight and conversion. The two disciples plodded on, merely curious to hear more from this strange man; so they invited him to stay for supper. Only in the characteristic gesture of the blessing and breaking of the bread did they finally recognize him. He disappeared, and only then, with the benefit of hindsight, were they beginning to understand: 'Were not our hearts burning within us while he was talking to us on the road, while he was opening the scriptures to us?' The Emmaus episode tells us (among many other things) that even intellectual insight — understanding mentally what Jesus taught — does not automatically lead to spiritual insight — understanding what it involves and means for one's own life. On the other hand, among those who refused to accept Jesus' own image of himself, who denied it because it did not fit their religious, social and political agenda, conversions have taken place and continue to take place. Paul is the first example in the history of the church. T.S. Eliot and C.S. Lewis are among the better-known cases in the twentieth century. Jesus had no illusions about this. 'Oh, how foolish you are,' he tells the Emmaus disciples, 'and how slow of heart to believe all that the prophets have declared.' And he knew of course that no academic exercise, no historical analysis of his words or those of his opponents, would force anyone to believe in him. If even the two Emmaus disciples, listening to the risen Christ himself, merely felt their hearts burning before they finally recognized him, not because of his words but through a gesture, we should humbly accept that Jesus was and is more than our minds can grasp. And we should also understand that he himself clearly knew who he was. Occasionally, he may have told his disciples and those healed by him not to divulge his messianic miracles and his messiahship to anyone else, because he knew that this would alert opponents too soon. But he did perform miracles and preach sermons, and he was identifiable to those who had eyes to see and ears to hear (cf. Mark 8:18).

Mark, the oldest of the Gospel writers, and John, with his uniquely personal perspective, along with Matthew and Luke, agree that Jesus used a specific form of address when talking about himself: 'I am...' This is not quite as innocuous as it sounds. The Greek texts have *Ego eimi*, and the use of *ego*, which is not necessary in Greek grammar, stresses the imperative nature of the claim: '*I* am...' In Hebrew and Aramaic, the same emphasis is apparent: *Ani hu*. The Torah introduces it, in Deuteronomy 5:6–7: 'I am the Lord, your God, who brought you out of the land of Egypt, out of the house of slavery; you shall have no other gods besides me.' Or look at Deuteronomy 32:39: 'See now that I, even I, am he; there is no God besides me. I kill and I make alive, I wound and I heal; and no one can deliver from my hand.' At the Feast of Tabernacles, or Sukkoth, a verse from Isaiah was recited: 'You are my witnesses, says the Lord, and my servant whom I have chosen, so that you may know and believe me and understand that I am he' (Isaiah 43:10). These are just some examples. Furthermore, as a rule the Greek translation of the Hebrew Bible, the so-called Septuagint, which was produced by Jews for Jews in the third/second centuries before Christ, translates the Hebrew *ani hu* into the Greek *ego eimi*, so that even the Greek-speaking Jews and Jewish Christians were able to understand the allusion in the Gospels. If Jesus uses this emphatic formula to speak about himself, the message is clear: 'It is me – I am God incarnate.'

An early instance occurs in Mark 6:45–52. There was a storm on the lake. The disciples were struggling against the adverse wind, and Jesus, who had been alone on the land, approached them, walking on the lake. 'They thought it was a ghost and cried out; for they all saw him and were terrified. But immediately he spoke to them and said: "Take heart, it is I; do not be afraid."' This is the formula again, *ego eimi*, in Mark's Greek, or *ani hu*, if we translate it into Hebrew. John confirms this account in his Gospel (6:16–21; see also Matthew 14:22–27), and again we read the words of God's appearance among his people: 'It is I, do not be afraid – *ego eimi, ani hu*.' Just as with the expression 'son of man', people could circumnavigate the intended meaning and hear a simple 'I am Jesus,' but the situation as such was obvious enough. The formula, with the emphasis on the 'I', could only be missed by people 'whose hearts were hardened' (Mark 6:52) or whose eyes would be opened at a later stage. The opponents of Jesus did not miss the point, though. Words like 'I and the

Father are One' were sufficient for them to try to stone him to death. Caiaphas tore his clothes when Jesus pronounced the 'It is me' formula and treats this as sufficient evidence for a blasphemy that demands the death penalty (Mark 14:62–64). Luke reports that Jesus used the words in his first resurrection appearance to the (male) disciples in Jerusalem, after the Emmaus episode: 'They were startled and terrified, and thought that they were seeing a ghost. He said to them: "Why are you frightened, and why do doubts arise in your heart? Look at my arms and my feet; see that it is me"' (Luke 24:37–39). Again it is helpful to note the emphatic Greek: *Ego eimi autós*. The last word marks a Jewish translation of the *Ani hu* into ancient Greek – 'I am it,' or 'I am he myself.'

There is no room for doubt. Jesus claimed to be the Messiah, the Son of God and God himself. He had said so all along, using this formula at regular intervals (see also John 13:19 with Isaiah 42:8 and 43:10). Some understood it immediately, many did after the resurrections, and many more have understood it during the past two millennia. Others still fail to see this truth and occasionally even try to explain it away, as though Jesus had never said it. But the sources are adamant. Jesus was handed over to Pontius Pilate not least for this unique and powerful claim. The one thing Caiaphas and his henchmen – who by no means represented the majority of Jews – did not need was this man who threatened their power structure and their delicate relationship with the corrupt Roman prefect. To them, he was an embarrassment and a danger. To his followers ever since, he was and remains the saviour.

Over and against all this evidence, those who think Jesus was just a good man and a charismatic leader are hopelessly out of touch. The 'good man' option never existed. Of those who knew him, the opponents and enemies saw him as a blasphemer, the Roman prefect crucified him as a criminal who had committed *lèse-majesté* (treason), but his followers acknowledged him as the Messiah, Son of God and redeemer: there never was a middle way. It is of course true that he was also a charismatic leader, but this really is an 'also'; as the new Moses, he showed comparable qualities. Unlike Moses, though, he did not see charismatic leadership as his God-given purpose. His charisma, and his charismatic gifts, were elements of his personality, not its essence. In fact, as people like C.S. Lewis have said before, Jesus either spoke the truth and was who he said he was, or he was the most adept liar, a manipulator who led people astray. The historical evidence of course points the way towards the first characterization. Whether we walk that way remains our personal decision. God has given us the free will to deny or to accept his invitation: 'If you continue in my word, you are truly my disciples; and you will know the truth, and the truth will make you free.' (John 8:31–32).

9

MODERN CHOICES

Gifted teacher, Cynic philosopher, God, myth or man?

In the previous chapter, we saw how Jesus' contemporaries either challenged or accepted his self-image and the grounds on which they did so. As many of us today have to grapple with various images of Jesus presented to us by the world, opening windows to let in the past may not be all that helpful. Looking for answers to help us shape our own lives, we may not always find comfort in the experiences of people from two thousand years ago. On the other hand, it is plain that a God who acts with history in mind would not haven chosen the Roman province of Syria, with Galilee, Samaria and Judea, at precisely that moment in time without a purpose – and that therefore the quest for ever deeper insights into this world is not an academic's pastime but is eminently necessary if we intend to take God seriously. For our daily needs, however, such a quest may seem superfluous. What, after all, does Jesus mean to us here and now? As a consequence, people in modern times, far removed from eyewitnesses and their reactions, tend to create their own ideas about Jesus. Unfortunately, precisely because these people are removed from Jesus' origins, such ideas often become arbitrary and emotional. Such thinking often requires making the risky ideological decision that the classical sources, particularly those of the Gospels and the other writings collected in the New Testament, can be largely discounted. For only if you make yourself the master of the texts, rather than their attentive servant, will you be able to discard those aspects that do not fit into your own picture. Classical philologists and historians know that it is illegitimate to force a given text into shape by cutting off what you do not like and stretching to breaking point whatever you might need for your particular theories. Such attempts will destroy the texts, and you will be left with the outpourings of your own imagination, rather than the message of the documents. Texts from antiquity, written in distant times, demand patience and humility, and it may take years of research rather than a casual throw of the dice to establish what an ancient author and his earliest readers knew.

In some cases recently, tendencies among Jesus scholars have verged on the extreme. Just one example is the endeavours of the so-called 'Jesus Seminar', a worldwide fraternity of people originating in the United States around people like Robert Funk, Dominic Crossan, Burton Mack and Marcus Borg. It has become infamous far beyond scholarly circles, thanks to a ballot system that decides whether words of Jesus in the Gospels are authentic, just about possible or plainly invented. The passages chosen in this supposedly democratic but entirely wanton way – after all, New Testament research is not a general election, but an academic process of painstaking analysis – are then marked in colours corresponding to the decision. It comes as no surprise that the like-minded arch-liberals who got together to cast beads into the ballot machine found hardly anything in John's Gospel to be authentic. Having made a laughing stock of themselves, they continued to produce books that claimed rather weird things about Jesus. In one case, he was a Cynic philosopher, but in a later book, the same scholar then changed his mind and turned Jesus into a Jewish peasant, poor and dispossessed, but still a revolutionary sage, with a narrow vision of the here and now. This is fiction, entirely unrelated to everything we know about the historical Jesus and his teaching about himself. But unfortunately, such works have become fashionable and highly quotable for anyone who needs the voice of a university professor to 'prove' that even Christian scholars no longer believe that Christ was Christ. Many members of the Jesus Seminar seem to be convinced that they can let their fantasies run wild on the basis of an early source, 'Q' (which stands for the German *Quelle*, or 'source') – which, as philologists know, never existed – and on the basis of later writings, composed between the mid-second and late-fourth centuries, such as the so-called gospels of Peter and Thomas. The latter is not a gospel of Thomas at all, but a collection of sayings that avoid anything that might come close to the suffering, crucifixion and bodily resurrection of Jesus.

Those who read such outpourings are reminded of the many heresies that sprang up in the latter part of the second century. Offended by the stark message of the New Testament, people like the docetists taught that Jesus was only seemingly a man — therefore, he only seemingly suffered on the cross. Around 320 AD, a man called Arius nearly changed the course of church history when he claimed that Jesus was not truly God incarnate, but a separate being of a lesser status. The Council of Nicea, convened by Emperor Constantine in AD 325, settled the matter with the first creed, which confirmed that Jesus was identical with God the Father. But Arianism survived and has made a reappearance in some circles of modern theology. Anyone studying the history of the church during the first five centuries will marvel at the efforts made at that time to invent a Jesus figure who might be palatable to Greek philosophers and other pagan thinkers. The whole world of the so-called 'Gnosis', a technical term that describes all these movements but simply means 'insight' or 'knowledge', is a tangle of detours and convoluted escape routes, all of them trying to get away from the historical Jesus. Names like Valentinian or Marcion, or collections like the *Corpus Hermeticum*, discovered at Nag Hammadi in Egypt in 1946, fascinated scholars who wanted to know more about the critical centuries when authentic church teachers such as Ireneus of Lyon, Clement of Alexandria, Hippolytus and others battled for the truth of the Gospels. But these movements also attracted people who found the message of the New Testament uncomfortably challenging — after all, it is not about a philosophy, but about a radical commitment that involves penitence and obedience to God. The gnostic writers offered a convenient way around this insight by omitting the uncomfortable aspects and praising the celebration of mystic knowledge. This could be celebrated on one's own or in communion with others, and would feel cosy rather than challenging. Soul-searching was out, mind-searching was in. Paul, who was a clever, highly intellectual man – anyone's match as far as Greek philosophy and Jewish theology were concerned – warned against such tendencies, but his words were not always heeded. He saw the signs in other areas, too. When Christians celebrated *Agape*, or 'love meals', and drank themselves stupid with wine instead of celebrating Holy Communion in memory of Jesus' sacrifice as he had instructed them to do, something was clearly beginning to go wrong.

Rebutting such theories and practices, the early Christian thinkers insisted that history and faith must not be separated. On the one hand, the historical truth of Jesus and his message is contained in the four authentic Gospels. Everything else is myth and should be rejected. Paul expressed a warning that is as topical today as it was then: 'For the time is coming when people will not put up with sound doctrine, but having itching ears, they will accumulate for themselves teachers to suit their own desires, and will turn away from listening to the truth and wander away to myths' (2 Timothy 4:3–4). And Peter said it in his second letter: 'For we did not follow cleverly devised myths when we made known to you the power and coming of our Lord Jesus Christ, but we had been eyewitnesses of his majesty' (2 Peter 1:16; see also Chapter 2). Not to be outdone, those who do not like such straightforward utterances have subscribed to the theory that Peter did not write his second letter and that Paul did not write 2 Timothy. However, even if this was the case — and recent research has demonstrated that it is not — it remains early Christian teaching and an authoritative part of the New Testament.

On the other hand, beyond the rebuttal of myths by those who knew they had experienced historical truth, there is faith. Understanding and believing that Jesus is God incarnate and suffered for our sins, not seemingly, but really, is a statement of faith based on Jesus' own words. As we saw in the previous chapter, one may accept or reject it, but one cannot prove it wrong historically. Many of those who invented gnostic theories about Jesus against the early church, and many of those who continue to do so today, have forgotten that a coin has two sides and that it will lose its value if one of those sides is effaced or was never stamped in the first place. Equally, you can only see one of its sides at a time. When you look at the Jesus of history, it is him that you see, study and seek to understand. And when you look at the Christ of faith, converse with him in prayer and follow him as a real presence in your life, he is the one before your eyes. Whichever side of the coin you look at, you know that the other side is there. Deny one side, and the coin will lose all value and credibility. One cannot buy anything with a valueless half coin.

Modern fantasy pictures of Jesus hardly ever add anything new — in fact, they are a constant reminder of the verdict in the book of Ecclesiastes in the Old Testament: 'There is nothing new under the sun. Is there a thing of which it is said, "See, this is new"? It has already been, in

JESUS, MAN OR MYTH?

the ages before us.' (Ecclesiastes 1:9–10). For example,
the Jesus Seminar and their home-made mythical world
inhabited by an evangelist, John, who is entirely of their
own making, a Gospel author who allegedly invented the
words, teachings and prayers of Jesus, is matched by the
sectarian movement of the Alogi in the second century.
They rejected the Gospel's historical and doctrinal value,
and ascribed it to someone called Cerinthus. A certain
Gaius had followers who rejected John because they
disliked his comments on the Holy Spirit and feared they
encouraged another sectarian movement, the so-called
Montanists. In other words, fiddling with the evidence
because it does not fit in with one's own thought system
is an ancient practice. Such schools of thought were dealt
with by early scholars like Hippolytus, who wrote a
powerful 'Defence of the Gospel According to St John and
the Apocalypse' as early as about AD 200. Even the habit
of deleting, adding or changing textual passages to suit
one's ideology is not new, although it must be given to the
Jesus Seminar that they have gone to innovative extremes
with the idea of dropping beads into a ballot box to decide
which of Jesus' words are authentic. They may not yet have
dared to publish a New Testament where all the
'blackballed' passages are left out, but their procedure
amounts to the same. In earlier centuries, others simply
published new manuscripts to produce the desired effect.
Just one example follows.

The real Jesus, who truly suffered, expressed his sense of
forlornness and dereliction in heart-rending words. He did
so as a Jew, in Jewish terminology. On the cross, he quoted
the first line of of Psalm 22, 'My God, my God, why have

you forsaken me?' This was the psalmist's – his forefather David's – moment of feeling abandoned by God. The moment soon passed, as Psalm 22 explains, and it ends in the messianic triumph of being with God eternally and living forever. But although the feeling passed as soon as it came, it was undeniably there. God himself spoke about such moments in Isaiah: 'For a brief moment, I abandoned you, but with great compassion I will gather you' (Isaiah 54:7). And yet, in spite of this passage and in spite of the message of the complete Psalm 22, there have always been readers of the New Testament who did not like the directness of verses that hit us with the insight into a Jesus suffering in loneliness. Forgetting that Jesus was both fully God and fully man, they cannot stomach the reality of the pain he endured as a human being, both physically and mentally. And thus, such passages were tampered with in several manuscripts. In the case of the quote from Psalm 22, it was slightly more difficult to alter the evidence, as it was quoted in both Mark 15:34 and Matthew 27:46, and not in Greek but in Aramaic, the everyday language of Jesus and most Jews in the Holy Land. Those who dared to change the text could do so only if they assumed that the readers would not be able to check it against the Aramaic. Even so, some manuscript copies of Mark's Gospel substituted 'Why have you forsaken me?' with 'Why have you reproached me?' Whoever did it was a scribe in official employ, and he deleted the moment of most abject loneliness from the text.

'Correctors' were less inhibited when they manipulated another exclamation of suffering and anguish. In Luke 23:43-44 we read: 'Then an angel from heaven appeared to him and gave him strength. In his anguish he prayed more earnestly, and his sweat became like great drops of blood falling down on the ground.' Here, the squeamishness set in much earlier and more forcefully. Two papyri, five codices, several ancient translations and theologians such as Clement of Alexandria and Origen of Caesarea (plus the heretic Marcion) deleted these two verses. They did not even try to put anything in their place. As it happens, we have the voices of early authors such as Justin, Irenaeus and Hippolytus, who intimate that these sentences were in the text originally, but the widespread evidence for their deletion has made some scholars uncertain to this day. A final case in point: 'We do see Jesus, who for a little while was made lower than the angels, now crowned with glory and honour because of the suffering of death, so that apart from God he might taste death for everyone' (Hebrews 2:9). This is the original text. It echoes Psalm 22:1, but it proved indigestible to many readers and copyists. They simply changed the Greek *chôrìs theou*, 'apart from God' or 'without God', into *cháriti theou*, 'by the grace of God'. And this is how we read it in all modern translations – thankfully, some at least offer an explanatory footnote in which the original text can be found.

As in the previous case, a sizeable number, in fact the majority of existing manuscripts, have the 'grace' reading. But as philologists and textual critics know, majority is not a criterion in deciding between different readings – nor are there 'good' or 'bad' papyri. There are only right or wrong readings. Even a supposedly good papyrus may contain one or several wrong readings. A later manuscript, even if it stands completely on its own today, may well preserve the correct, original text. And indeed, things can change. Origen, studying the manuscript evidence for the whole Greek Bible in the early third century, knew that the vast majority had 'apart from God'. By the time of Jerome in the late fourth/early fifth century, the situation had changed. Now the majority read 'by the grace of God'. Something must have happened. But what? It is obvious that the second reading was introduced, preferred and successfully imposed for dogmatic reasons – to such an extent that only three manuscripts have survived today that preserve the ancient original. Christ without God was not politically correct, and once the church was powerful enough to influence the manuscript tradition, under and after Emperor Constantine (who ruled from AD 312 to 336), these alterations became feasible. Anyone who reads the altered text carefully, though, will wonder how it can be 'a *grace* of God' that Christ suffered on the cross. Desperate to get the separation from God out of the text, and trying to choose a different word that looked vaguely similar in Greek, the falsifiers weakened the powerful language of the letter to the Hebrews. The original word is consistent with the overall message of this letter and with Mark 15:34 and Matthew 27:46 – and yet it was sacrificed to a new theology.

Thus, modern theologians who shape their own Jesus according to their own theologies and ideologies are merely following in ancient footsteps. The list of examples could be extended at leisure. Even today, manipulation of the actual text remains a possibility. What, for example, did Jesus teach his disciples about the prerequisites for the expulsion of demons? Apart from the fact that some New

Testament critics prefer to doubt that there were (and are) demons and that Jesus cast them out, the case is clear. In cases of life-threatening danger, when the whole of one's existence, body, mind and soul, is possessed, it follows that the healer's body, mind and soul must be prepared to face the enemy. 'This kind can come out only through prayer and fasting,' Jesus explains to the disciples who had failed to cast out the demon (Mark 9:29). For anyone who has tried to understand Jewish thought, this is a logical consequence. Jesus does not depart radically from the Jewish concept of body, mind and soul as a whole, created by God – he emphasizes it. Praying and fasting generally characterize Jews who want to be ready for God. 'There was also a prophet, Anna the daughter of Phanuel, of the tribe of Asher,' we read in Luke 2:36–37. 'She was of great age, having lived with her husband for seven years after her marriage, then as a widow to the age of eighty-four. She never left the temple but worshipped there with fasting and prayer night and day.' In Antioch, Barnabas and Paul are to be commissioned by the community, and everyone gets ready: 'After fasting and prayer, they laid their hands on them and sent them off' (Acts 13:3). Barnabas and Paul themselves later followed the same practice: 'And after they had appointed elders for them in each church, with prayer and fasting they entrusted them to the Lord in whom they had come to believe' (Acts 14:23). Fasting is not always a continuous activity. It may be brief, just like a short but intense prayer. And fasting may also be wrong – Jesus criticized some of the Pharisees for their public, showpiece way of fasting, and recommended that his disciples fast in their own rooms, not in public. So much is obvious, then. The teaching of Jesus did not go beyond the scope of Jewish practice, but he applied it to a rarer activity, the casting out of demons.

Now open a New Testament, and you will find that practically all recent translations have deleted the fasting from Mark 9:29. You may find it in the footnotes, but as we saw briefly in a previous chapter, it has disappeared from the actual text. Why? Because the two standard editions of the Greek New Testament, the United Bible Societies text and Nestle-Aland, do not have it any more, and these are used and followed by translators. And what are the reasons for this radical departure from almost two thousand years of tradition? They are explained in the official handbook on the committee decisions that created the modern Greek text, Bruce Metzger's *Commentary on the Greek New Testament*. There we are told that 'in the light of the increasing emphasis in the early church on the necessity of fasting, it is understandable that "and by fasting" (*kai nêsteía* in the Greek) is a gloss that found its way into most witnesses.' This is ideology, or, if you prefer, bad theology, and it is certainly very bad textual criticism. Because of some guesswork about the alleged increase in fasting in the early church, it is decreed that these decisive words were added to the ancient manuscripts by fasting fanatics.

In fact, though, the early church had nothing to do with it — as we have seen, Jesus the teacher taught within the framework of Jewish thought and used fasting in a particular, extreme situation. He, and later his disciples through him, had the power to cast out demons. Others had not. But even the disciples could not just flick a switch to make it happen. They had to be prepared. Therefore, the few and late manuscripts of Mark's Gospel that deleted the fasting probably did so for quite another theological reason. It was not explicitly mentioned that Jesus had fasted before he went up the Mount of the Transfiguration (the incident immediately before the healing), and so they deleted it, forgetting that the transfiguration in Mark 9:2–8 was one of those cases where Jesus would have fasted beforehand anyway. The Gospels do not always go into detail about the obvious. One could even argue, turning Metzger's argument on its head, that 'and by fasting' was deleted because too many people had taken to fasting in the fourth century (when the deletion occurred), and the words were dropped so as not to encourage others. Whatever the reason, the text simply does not make sense without its punchline, the combination of prayer and fasting. Praying was something the disciples would have done anyway before they tried to heal the demon-possessed boy. It went without saying. If this had been all Jesus had taught them after their failure, they would have stood there with blank incomprehension. In brief, even Jesus the teacher can be manipulated by modern editorial decisions, and as a result, he may lose both his Jewishness and the reach of his timeless teaching.

In a world that was shaped by Greco-Roman influences which permeated even the Jewish everyday world of Jesus, it was essential for him to be seen as a Jew among Jews, and as the fulfilment of Jewish messianic expectations. This was the first challenge, as hardly any Jew — his own disciples included — expected someone who would teach, act, suffer, die and rise in the way he did. At the same time,

Jesus was also the first Jewish teacher to reach out to non-Jews. 'Salvation comes from the Jews,' he explained (John 4:22) when he went into Syro-Phoenician territory. He visited the eastern Decapolis; he performed a miracle, the feeding of the multitudes, twice — first for five thousand Jews, then for four thousand non-Jews on the eastern shores of the Lake of Galilee; he healed a demon-possessed man in Greek-speaking Roman territory near Gadara; and he chose the site for his messianic proclamation by Peter, at Caesarea Philippi, near the shrine of the Greek god Pan and the temple of the god-emperor Augustus, where the central river of the Jewish homeland, the Jordan, rises from the rocks. This Jesus was multilingual. As we know today, he spoke fluent Hebrew as well as Aramaic and Greek — the international language of communication. He cannot be honed to fit into isolated strands within Jewish theology or Greco-Roman philosophy, let alone to fit the mindset of a Galilean peasant or a social revolutionary. Why then should it make sense to see Jesus as a proto-feminist or a pseudo-Essene, an early psychoanalyst, an esoteric mystic or whatever else may have been dreamt up about him in recent times?

As we have seen throughout this book, real people in a real world are quite capable of speaking for themselves. Could it be that a modern picture of Jesus emerges if we return to one of his contemporaries, a man whom we encountered briefly before — Nicodemus? Let us try to find out what he can tell us. In his case, there was no mass audience, no public address, no gathering of four or five thousand — just the two of them, in an intimate conversation at night. This is how we first encounter

Nicodemus when he meets Jesus. John's Gospel introduces us to him at the beginning of chapter 3: 'Now there was a Pharisee named Nicodemus, a leader of the Jews. He came to Jesus by night.' Why does John tell us who Nicodemus was? After all, you might argue that the teaching that follows is of universal and eternal value, not just of personal interest to a single man. Yes indeed, and that is why it is recorded so carefully in this Gospel. One of the two must have passed the information on to the disciples. Nicodemus could have done so after the burial and resurrection of Jesus – remember that he was with Joseph of Arimathea when they buried Jesus and embalmed him with myrrh and aloe. But as readers of John's Gospel know, this evangelist means what he says and is at pains to record those little details that he considers important. Nicodemus was a Pharisee: in other words, he belonged to one of the three major Jewish movements of the time. There is no trace anywhere in the Gospels of an outright condemnation of all Pharisees or of an uncompromising rejection of all their tenets. In fact, we encounter a rather positive portrayal of another leading Pharisee – Gamaliel – later, in the book of Acts. There is no reason to assume that Jesus mistrusted Nicodemus. He was a Pharisee – fine, now let's find out how eager to listen and learn he really was.

Nicodemus was 'a leader of the Jews'. In other words – and John 7:45–52 underlines this observation – he was a member of the Sanhedrin, the highest Jewish council, led by the high priest. He represented the elite of Jewish society. And such a man wanted to debate with Jesus. Why then did he come to Jesus by night? Was he afraid his colleagues might see him and ostracize him for visiting the controversial wandering rabbi from Nazareth? Far from it. In those days, all deeper questions of theology and philosophy were pondered and discussed after sunset. It is a practice we encounter as early as Psalm 119:148, and thus it could be seen as a mark of respect to visit Jesus by night. Nicodemus takes this man seriously, treating him as an equal, in fact as more than an equal, for above all, he wants to listen and learn.

It is quite possible that Nicodemus was one of those leading Jews who had ancestors from the 'diaspora' – the dispersion of the Jews to foreign countries or from regions of the homeland that had long been permeated by Greek culture – as his name is Greek, not Hebrew: Nico-Demos, the victor (*nikos*) of the people (*demos*). It seems that there is a Hebrew derivative of the name, 'Nakdimon', but John insists on the Greek name and Nakdimon has a different meaning anyway, 'the sun has broken through'. However, given the typical upbringing of such high-ranking, Hellenized Jews, conversant with Greek literature and philosophy (without denying or downplaying the supremacy of the Torah, of course), we may even assume that he saw himself rather like one of those men who met with the Greek philosopher Socrates, asked questions and provided the cues for the teacher's insights. In any case, we should take careful note of what he says right at the beginning of their conversation: 'Rabbi, we know you are a teacher who has come from God; for no one can do these signs that you do apart from the presence of God.' Other Pharisees, from different schools of thought, would have seen Jesus in a completely different light. But Nicodemus meant what he said, and Jesus knew it. The whole conversation is marked by a sincere quest for eternal truth.

The fact that Jesus assumes sound biblical and theological learning on the part of his listener is apparent throughout. There is, for example, the reference to an incident taken from the Torah, the five books of Moses, which were and are the cornerstone of the Jewish faith. The Israelites were in the wilderness. They were dying. They were threatened by poisonous snakes. Moses made a bronze snake and lifted it up on a pole. Anyone who looked at it was healed (Numbers 21:9). So far, so familiar. But there was also a Jewish text written in the period between the Old and New Testaments that never made it into the canon of scripture, the so-called Wisdom of Solomon from the mid-second century BC. It calls this bronze snake a 'symbol of salvation' (Wisdom 16:6). Undoubtedly, a learned man like Nicodemus would have known both the Torah and the Wisdom of Solomon. Without Jesus explaining it in so many words, Nicodemus would have been aware of a lasting and healing message behind the ancient act of Moses. What Nicodemus did not know and could not yet know was the deeper meaning of Jesus' comparison. 'Just as Moses lifted up the serpent in the wilderness, so must the Son of Man be lifted up, that whoever believes in him may have eternal life.' (John 5:14). Nicodemus knows about the Son of Man — from the description of the Messiah, mainly in the prophetic book of Daniel. He understands that Jesus sees himself as this Messiah.

In fact, Jesus leaves him in no doubt at all. A sentence later, he speaks of himself as the Son of God, and later still, as the only Son of God. In other words, he confirms and reinforces the introductory declaration of the Pharisee, 'You are a teacher who has come from God.' If Jesus must be lifted up like the bronze serpent of Moses in the wilderness, at a time of mortal danger to the Jews, then Jesus is a new sign in another wilderness, a spiritual desert where his fellow Jews are in danger of eternal perdition. Such signs and words would have remained earthbound, as it were, without the new and final meaning given to them by Jesus being 'lifted up'. For as we know today, and as Nicodemus was to learn a couple of years later, on Good Friday, 7 April AD 30, Jesus had to be lifted up on the cross. The bronze snake lifted up by Moses brought healing to the Jews in the wilderness. Jesus, who had come from the wilderness where he had prepared himself by forty days of fasting and praying, brought healing to the Jews and to all humankind by his death on the cross. It was to be a healing that was not confined to a momentary experience in the desert of the ancient Israelites but an everlasting healing that became the source of eternal life.

At this point in their conversation Jesus does not expect another question from Nicodemus. He knows that Nicodemus will have to wait for that hour by the cross before he can understand fully, and when he will act fittingly by burying Jesus with a royal amount of ointments 'weighing about a hundred pounds' (John 19:39). This is truly a gesture of veneration, and all the more remarkable as Nicodemus does this after Jesus' cruel death but before the glorious resurrection of this one and only Son of God. In fact, Nicodemus was not unprepared.

He had thought about the encounter with Jesus and enters the stage a second time, between the initial conversation and the burial, when he defends the Torah, and Jesus' teaching based on it, against a one-sided interpretation. 'Our law does not judge people without giving them a hearing to find out what they are doing, does it?' he says, and receives the arrogant reply of people who are too lazy to think: 'Surely you are not also from Galilee, are you? Search and you will see that no prophet is to arise from Galilee' (John 7:45–52).

Many scholars have doubted that Nicodemus could have gone, with Joseph of Arimathea, to bury Jesus with such an extravagant amount of myrrh and aloe. The biblical connotation is undeniable: myrrh and aloe were mentioned together in Psalm 45:8. But they also served the practical purpose of preventing the corpse from smelling (cf. John 11:39). 'About one hundred pounds,' or, correctly in Greek, nearly (*hôs*) one hundred *litras* (one of which equalled 326 grams) would have cost a fortune, and Nicodemus could hardly have transported this to the site without being noticed. Indeed, it was a huge amount, but it was certainly within the means of a wealthy Pharisee and definitely appropriate if Nicodemus intended to bury Jesus like a king, in a true believer's application of those mocking words composed by Pontius Pilate for the headboard above the cross, 'King of the Jews'. At the death of Gamaliel the Elder, the teacher of Paul (Acts 22:3) who also appears in Acts 5:33–39, a certain Onkelos burned eighty pounds of spices. Onlookers accused him of extravagance. He replied, referring to a passage in Jeremiah: ' "You shall die in peace, and with the burnings of your fathers who were before you." Is not Rabbi Gamaliel far better than a hundred kings?' Apparently, like Onkelos burying Gamaliel, Nicodemus had come to the conclusion that Jesus was far more important than any ancient king of the Jews. His spices are anything but a later legendary element invented by John the Evangelist.

Nicodemus appears in no further scenes in John's Gospel, nor anywhere else in the New Testament. Later traditions tell the story of his baptism by Peter and Paul. Legends talk of his persecution by other members of the Sanhedrin. The apocryphal 'Gospel of Nicodemus', originally called the 'Acts of Pilate', of the third/fourth century, informs its readers that Nicodemus and Joseph of Arimathea founded the church at Lydda (modern-day Lod). The Italian city of Parma claims to preserve some of his remains. Another Italian legend links a portrait of Jesus carved by Nicodemus with the cathedral of St Martin at Lucca. He was made a saint and is venerated on 3 August. Like those of most of the original twelve disciples, however, his post-biblical activities were probably known to his contemporaries, but, as they were part and parcel of the general flow of missionary activities, they were left unreported. He had served his primary purpose as a historical Pharisee who had learned from Jesus and changed his ways, defending the rabbi from Nazareth and courageously paying him the highest possible honour by giving him a royal burial, two days before the resurrection revealed Jesus' true messianic glory. He acted, and his act made him a role model for all those who watch and wait for others to take the first step.

In fact, the courage and dedication displayed by

Nicodemus may be seen as an early yardstick for discipleship. Here was a man who could think, who knew his myths from his prophecies and his historical facts, who kept an open mind, was eager to learn and resistant to peer pressure, and who was finally ready to risk his career in the humble act of honouring Jesus with a royal burial after he had just been crucified by the Romans like a common criminal. The usual suspects among New Testament critics have found this message too conveniently theological to be true and have decreed that Nicodemus never existed. We know better and appreciate him as a historical figure who learned by listening and observing, and who acted according to his insights into the truth lived and proclaimed by Jesus. Nicodemus is a role model for all who want to return to the sources, to think for themselves and to rediscover the Jesus of history and the Christ of faith behind the smokescreen of modernist rejection. There still is so much to discover. Archaeology, the study of coins, papyri, inscriptions — all these add to our knowledge. In some areas of research, the surface has only just been scratched. As with a mosaic, we enjoy a colourful picture when all the tesserae are in place. The mosaic of Jesus, fully man and fully God, not myth but truth personified, has been preserved in the writings of the New Testament. Trusting the image that this unique collection of sources gives us is the safest way towards an unhindered encounter with Jesus Christ today.

All Lion Books are available from your local bookshop, or can be ordered via our website or from Marston Book Services. For a free catalogue, showing the complete list of titles available, please contact:

Customer Services
Marston Book Services
PO Box 269
Abingdon
Oxon
OX14 4YN

Tel: 01235 465500
Fax: 01235 465555

Our website can be found at:
www.lionhudson.com